HACKING
GROUP WORK

11 Ways to Build Student Engagement, Accountability, and Cooperation with Collaborative Teams

HACK™
Learning
SERIES

CONNIE
HAMILTON

Hacking Group Work
© 2023 by Times 10 Publications
Highland Heights, OH 44143 USA
Website: 10publications.com

All rights reserved. It is illegal to reproduce copies of this work in print or
electronic format (including reproductions displayed on a secure intranet
or stored in a retrieval system or other electronic storage device from which
copies can be made or displayed) without the prior written permission
of the publisher, except by a reviewer, who may quote brief passages in a
review. For information regarding permission, contact the publisher at
mark@10publications.com. Times 10 Publications books are available at
special discounts when purchased in quantity for premiums, promotions,
fundraising, and educational use. For inquiries and details, contact us at
10publications.com.

All web links in this book are correct as of the publication date but may have
become inactive or otherwise modified since that time.

Cover and Interior Design by Steven Plummer
Editing by Regina Bell
Copyediting by Jennifer Jas
Project Management by Jen Z. Marshall

Paperback ISBN: 978-1-956512-37-3
eBook ISBN: 978-1-956512-40-3
Hardcover ISBN: 978-1-956512-39-7

Library of Congress Cataloging-in-Publication Data is available for this title.

First Printing: June 2023

Thank you to the thousands of teachers who opened their classrooms to me so we could discover together how minor tweaks can make a big difference in student learning.

Gratitude to Jennifer Gonzalez, editor of *Cult of Pedagogy* and author of this book's foreword, for the encouragement to make *Hacking Group Work* a reality.

Most of all, adoration and appreciation to my three adult children, Trey, Luke, and Allie. I love you most of all, and I said it first!

TABLE OF CONTENTS

FOREWORD

N A 2021 interview on my podcast, *The Cult of Pedagogy Podcast* (episode 172), Connie Hamilton was sharing one small, simple idea for improving group work. It was a strategy for empowering students who often feel as if they have little to contribute. I was so struck by the brilliance and originality of this one idea that I paused the interview mid-topic to point out that Connie really has a gift … she can take a five-second moment in a classroom and turn it into something that has a huge impact. Then I added, "I think the next thing you write needs to be a book about group work."

This is that book. And it's just as good as I thought it would be.

Collaboration is more important now than ever. We're living in a time when technology can replicate so many of the tasks we need to do in a day. This frees up time for humans to focus on the things only humans can do—communicating effectively, solving complex problems with creative solutions, and collaborating with others. Sharing space and synergizing are among the most exquisite things we can do together, and it's worth the effort to get it right.

But there's another, more important reason to give time to collaborative tasks: connection. As our society grows more accustomed to screens, many people have become less comfortable in social situations and more likely to avoid interacting with others. That's an alarming trend; for our mental and physical health, we have to reverse it.

We need to intentionally work at developing and nurturing our connections with each other. School is one place where students can practice the skills necessary to build those connections—guided, structured practice under the supervision of smart, caring adults. THAT is the value of classroom group work.

And this book will help you make the most of it.

Plenty of excellent materials about cooperative learning have already been published. Plenty of people have already contributed sound principles and guidelines that can help teachers implement effective collaborative practices in their classrooms. But a book by Connie Hamilton offers something different—it's like having a friend in the corner of your classroom, giving you a steady stream of smart, practical, instantly doable ideas that will make your teaching better.

Those ideas run the gamut from very small tweaks, such as providing a "parking lot" for student questions in order to minimize whole-class interruptions, to offering much deeper changes that address the emotional and cognitive factors that make group work so challenging. You'll find thoughtful insights on including introverted students in respectful ways, strategies for moving conversations past the surface level, and helpful moves on rehearsing classroom procedures to save time.

Far too often, we get teaching advice that may be inspiring but stops short of actually showing us HOW to accomplish a goal. *Hacking Group Work* is the opposite of that. As I read through it, I kept stopping to say, "Wait, I want to write that down. That's a great idea. People need to try this!" You could open this book to any page, read a few paragraphs, and find something you want to try tomorrow. And it would actually work.

If you have decided that optimizing your students' uniquely human skills is worth pursuing, I can say with confidence that Connie Hamilton will be a valuable companion along the way.

JENNIFER GONZALEZ
EDITOR, *CULT OF PEDAGOGY*

INTRODUCTION
I Loved It! I Hated It!

If you want to go fast, go alone. If you want to go far, go together.
— AFRICAN PROVERB

I HAD A LOVE-HATE relationship with group work when I was a student.

My ability to develop systems, organize tasks, and connect individuals to their areas of strength has come in handy throughout my career. When I think about how I developed those skills, I recall group projects when I led our team to create results that were better than any of us could have created individually. I loved checking criteria, delegating roles, and interacting with my peers. I had a vision for how it should work and took great pride when it did.

I loved it!

However, this wasn't always the case. Many times, I felt like I got stuck with unmotivated classmates who were happy to ride my coattails and share the same grade that I earned. I thought I coined the phrase, "If you want something done right, you have to do it yourself." Turns out that Napoleon said something similar. The leadership skills my mother so often pointed out to me triggered my inner perfectionist. Instead of the group working together in true collaboration, young Connie did the work of five students, as I recall.

I hated it!

When I became a teacher ... well, I can't say my perspective on group work changed much. I loved the days when students supported one another and I witnessed their "lightbulb" moments. You know what I mean: when students have a moment of clarity, often accompanied by "Oh! I get it now!" Glorious! These were the times when I knew my students were learning more than the standards; they were learning soft skills they'd need in the future to secure a job and grow in a career.

I loved it!

However, occasionally, groups didn't go as planned. Directions were not clear. Students communicated poorly. Some learners were off-task or stalled, and the quality of their work was mediocre at best. When it came time to assess individuals on what they had learned in their groups, it was painfully evident that the benefits of collaborative learning hadn't helped students reach their full potential for that unit. I worked harder than the students. Grading was nearly impossible and completely unfair. Some asked, "Why did the other kids get an A when I did all the work?" What could have been completed individually in a day took three days out of our valuable instructional time.

I hated it!

Now, as a school leader and consultant, I have observed hundreds—probably thousands—of student learning groups at work. Successful teachers have shared their secrets and, when things go amuck, their analysis of what went wrong. These examples have been invaluable for me to find problems and address them. My experiences as a student, teacher, and observer have provided valuable insights for these questions:

1. Why is it so important to include group work as a regular part of the learning process?

2. What are the common pitfalls that make group work a struggle for students and teachers?

3. How can we overcome challenges so group work allows students to collaborate with peers and holds them individually accountable for learning?

You Say Po-tay-to and I Say Po-tah-to

Throughout this book, I'll refer to group work as collaborative learning, student groups, learning teams, partner work, and groups. They are used interchangeably. For purposes of *Hacking Group Work*, they do not have nuanced differences in how they're defined, since different teachers have different ways of referencing their student groups.

Hone Your Hacking Skills

Hacking Group Work is intended to share answers to the three questions listed earlier so teachers can leverage the benefits of students learning from each other. The research is clear about the impact collaborative learning has on student success. When the machine doesn't feel well-oiled, it's tempting to label all group work as ineffective and return to teacher-centered lessons.

It's true that when the teacher does all the work, the work gets done. However, since our mission is for students to learn—not just for the test, but for life—then they must engage in learning tasks that challenge them. They must be unsuccessful at times and learn what doesn't work so that later they'll celebrate and gain confidence when they find a solution that does work, makes sense, or communicates clarity.

Breaking Down the Hacks

This book has been decades in the making through my teaching and consulting experiences. I selected the eleven problems I see most often in classrooms everywhere and share solutions that are practical, have been successful for other educators, and are rooted in research. Each chapter addresses one of these problems.

You may read the chapters in any sequence you'd like. Think of these Hacks as individual guides to overcoming the challenges that emerge when facilitating group work. I have purposefully flagged connections within the chapters to help you dig more deeply into an idea that is detailed in one Hack and simply referenced in another.

Within each chapter, I use the same Hack Learning Series template I used when writing *Hacking Homework* and *Hacking Questions*. Every chapter has seven sections. Feel free to jump around within a chapter to the sections you find most beneficial for your needs.

The Problem: This section describes in detail a challenge that teachers often face when facilitating group work. Each problem is chosen because it's common and poses a genuine obstacle for successful collaborative learning. The rest of the chapter is dedicated to solving the problem and offering readers everything they need to tackle it head-on and to achieve success.

The Hack: Hacks are simple, practical, and sometimes edgy ways to solve common problems in schools. This section describes a mindset, an approach, or a tool that offers a solution. You might find a different perspective that allows you to approach the problem from a different angle. Sometimes you will discover a strategy that prevents or reduces the likelihood that the problem will surface at all. Templates or tools might ease the difficulty of planning and fostering student-centered learning teams. Best of all, you'll have everything you need to apply the Hack.

What You Can Do Tomorrow: When faced with a problem, educators are often motivated to solve it. This section lists actions teachers can take immediately. The suggestions do not require extensive planning, funding, administrative approval, or anything that would prevent you from trying it out tomorrow. Many of my readers find this section the most valuable. It cuts to the chase and offers concrete and detailed suggestions for how you can take immediate action to overcome your challenges with group work.

A Blueprint for Full Implementation: Here is where the Hack is described step by step. It is a sequence of actions teachers can take in order to see the positive results of the solution. In true Hack Learning style, you will find the steps to be thorough and descriptive. Where appropriate, I provide the tools you need (including templates and resources) for free at my website, hackinggroupwork.com.

Overcoming Pushback: The authors of *Hacking Education*, the first Hack Learning Series book, are Mark Barnes (the CEO of Times 10 Publications) and Jennifer Gonzalez (you might know her from the *Cult of Pedagogy* podcast and blog or as the writer of this book's foreword). When they designed the template for the series, they included a section called Overcoming Pushback.

If I had been one of the founding authors, I might have labeled it the "Yeah, But" section. This is where we address objections based on legitimate concerns. When writing this section, I predicted what might be shared as a reason for the problem to remain unsolved. Excuses, rebuttals, concerns, issues, worries … anything that prevents teachers from developing effective student learning groups. Then the pushback, or Yeah, Buts, are answered with counter-arguments, mind shifts, additional solutions, or clear rationales.

The Hack in Action: When I'm partnering with schools, teachers often request to see a strategy in action. They want to know what it looks like with real students when they implement new instructional methods or learning approaches. Therefore, in this section, I describe a real classroom using the Hack to solve a problem.

You'll notice a wide variety of content areas and grade levels represented in the Hack in Actions. This is intentional. I am mindful that relevancy matters and readers are likely teaching K–12 in core or specialty areas. In the Hack in Action sections, the focus is on the Hack, not the curriculum or grade level. The solutions are universal and are helpful to teachers of students at all ages and in all subject areas. To make these Hacks even more flexible, I've included brief adaptations for an elementary example that can be tweaked to be successful with older students, and vice versa.

Summary: Since questioning is my passion, it seems fitting to punctuate each chapter with reflection and application questions. They are designed to help you sum up the key points of the chapter and begin thinking about how to apply each Hack in your classroom.

Templates, Tools, and Resources for You

Throughout the text, I reference over sixty protocols and learning structures. I've made them easy to find by using a unique style (such as Triad) when they appear in the text. Occasionally, descriptions are given within the text. No worries … I won't leave you wondering how you can use these activities. A complete list of all the protocols referenced in *Hacking Group Work* and their descriptions are available in the appendix.

You can also find tools to implement the protocols by visiting my website, hackinggroupwork.com, where you may download templates, posters, tools, and more. There's no cost: I offer them to you to enhance your experience with this book.

Please put them all to good use and share them widely.

Now Get Out There … But Come Visit

Now that you know the purpose of this book and how to get the most out of it, you're ready to get reading.

To reinforce and supplement what you learn here, I invite you to connect with me online and engage with other teachers who are reaping the benefits of effective group work. If you're engaged in a book study, however large or small, you're welcome to request access to a study guide on my website. The study guide is designed to prompt discourse among educators as you engage in thoughtful dialogue about the Hacks. The study guide is also free.

I'm excited to hear about your successes and will do my best to partner with you to solve any problems that are not addressed in the book. Check out the About the Author page at the end of this book for multiple ways to connect with me.

HACK 1

CALM THE AMYGDALA

Create a Sense of Safety

Worry does not empty tomorrow of its sorrow.
It empties today of its strength.
— CORRIE TEN BOOM, AUTHOR AND SPEAKER

THE PROBLEM: STUDENTS ARE THREATENED BY GROUP WORK

A HIGH SCHOOL SCIENCE teacher tweeted, "I have (a) good classroom community. Asking my HS kids to (do) group work today in random teams of 4 was like asking them to put pretzel salt in their eyes. One girl told me she hated it & I believe her. Some kids 100% shut down. Post Zoom is different. Is group work still essential?"

Kelly O'Connor was pleading for solutions to the first problem with group work: some students are threatened by group work and prefer to work alone. The replies to her tweet were a mixture of empathy and amazing suggestions. My response, like many of the other educators who read her tweet, was absolutely YES, group work is still essential.

So, if we know that developing communication skills and deepening learning are essential, how do we design collaborative learning to be less painful than pretzel salt in students' eyes?

Humans are social creatures. Oodles of research studies say collaborative group work is an effective method to support student learning. It has been proven over and over that when people engage with others, their learning, information retention, and overall success are greater than when working alone.

But this begs the question: If it's more effective to learn socially, why do so many students cringe at the idea of group work?

To maximize learning through human interactions, students need a social, emotional, and academic safe zone.

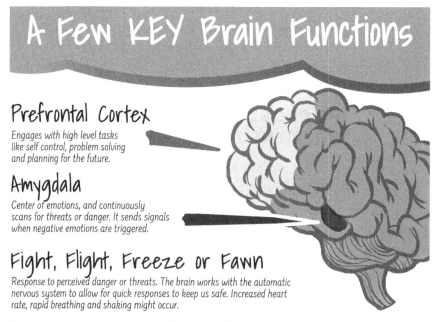

A Few KEY Brain Functions

Prefrontal Cortex
Engages with high level tasks like self control, problem solving and planning for the future.

Amygdala
Center of emotions, and continuously scans for threats or danger. It sends signals when negative emotions are triggered.

Fight, Flight, Freeze or Fawn
Response to perceived danger or threats. The brain works with the automatic nervous system to allow for quick responses to keep us safe. Increased heart rate, rapid breathing and shaking might occur.

These reactions to danger are automatic and can happen if the threat is real or perceived.

Image 1.1

Social workers and therapists who work with children help them understand how their brains function by introducing them to the idea of the brain as a guard dog, an ape, and a wise owl. These three parts of the brain have important functions that help us stay safe and make good decisions. They represent the amygdala (guard dog); the fight, flight, freeze, or fawn response (ape); and the prefrontal cortex (wise owl).

Here's how they work:

Amygdala: The part of the brain that never sleeps, as represented by a guard dog. The brain's guard dog is the center of emotions and continuously scans for possible danger. When negative emotions like fear, worry, anger, or despair are triggered, the amygdala does its job and goes on alert. The warning from the guard dog causes the fight, flight, freeze, or fawn response to kick in and prevents or delays the prefrontal cortex from doing its job.

Fight, Flight, Freeze, or Fawn Response: It's how the brain reacts to danger or threats, as represented by an ape. When the guard dog sounds off, it triggers the ape to take action. It works with the autonomic nervous system to release hormones that allow for quick responses to keep us safe:

- *Fight:* Your body prepares for the physical demands of fighting. You might experience anger or feel an urge to punch, kick, or attack something or someone.

- *Flight:* Hormones like adrenaline are released to prepare you to run longer and faster than you typically could. Conditions include fidgeting, constant movement of your limbs, dilating eyes, and restlessness.

- *Freeze:* Occurs when your body doesn't think it can fight or flight. In addition to experiencing a sense of dread, your heart pounds and you may feel stiffness, heaviness, or chills.

- *Fawn:* Happens when fight, flight, or freeze are unsuccessful and the threat remains. Prolonged exposure to this situation leads to over-agreement, pleasing others, and taking great measures to avoid conflict.

These reactions to danger are automatic and triggered whether the threat is real or perceived.

Prefrontal Cortex: It is best known for executive functioning and higher-level cognitive tasks, as represented by a wise owl. Self-control, decision-making, problem-solving, and planning for the future are all roles of the prefrontal cortex. When accessed, the prefrontal cortex helps the amygdala separate actual threats from perceived threats.

A chain reaction is set off in a student's brain when their amygdala senses threat. It doesn't have to be an actual threat; the amygdala doesn't have the ability to decipher real threats from perceived ones. This triggers the fight, flight, freeze, or fawn mode while simultaneously shutting down the prefrontal cortex. That's right! When the amygdala goes on alert, the person cannot engage in self-control, problem-solving, or decision-making. This comes in handy when you're facing a grizzly bear. You'll appreciate not having to develop a plan for survival because your body will take over in an effort to keep you safe. However, it's not so great in a group work setting.

This translates into the guard dog sensing danger and alerting the ape. In doing so, it scares off the owl who is nowhere to be found when the ape responds without thoughtful reflection. As long as the guard dog believes there is danger, the ape continues to respond without purposeful thought because the wise owl is temporarily silenced.

Over time, your brain calms down and the prefrontal cortex reengages, and the wise owl flies back. Sometimes it's a matter of seconds. For example, if you hear a loud noise, your amygdala senses danger, your body goes into flight mode, and without having to think about it, you duck and cover. When you realize it was just the wind slamming a door shut, that's your prefrontal cortex assuring your amygdala that you're actually safe. However, the impact lingers for a few minutes. Your heart is racing, your breathing is accelerated, and you might be shaky for a bit.

To maximize learning through human interactions, students need a social, emotional, and academic safe zone.

As educators, it's tempting to dismiss the notion that group work is threatening to students. But you can't replace a student's amygdala with their prefrontal cortex. When they sense danger, their amygdala treats everything as a real threat—even if it's perfectly harmless. In the slamming-door scenario, when there's evidence of what caused the loud sound, the threat is dismantled. In the case of a student who fears being made fun of, not being accepted, repeated negative experiences with group work, or a lack of confidence in their knowledge, the threat lingers. The amygdala is still sensing a threat. It might not be a physical threat, but the guard dog does not overlook social and emotional threats. As long as the student perceives a possibility that something bad could happen, their amygdala continues to be on high alert, and the prefrontal cortex is dormant.

THE HACK: CALM THE AMYGDALA

Students' aversions to group work cause some teachers to fight or flee themselves. Pushing the matter, continuing to put students in uncomfortable situations and hoping they'll change their minds about group work will not solve the problem. In fact, you'll be trading one smallish problem for a giant one because when students feel threatened by group work—meaning their social, emotional, or academic safety is in jeopardy—their amygdala awakens and they won't respond to your assurances or persuasion.

Other teachers throw their hands up when students repeatedly express their desire to work alone. They revert back to teacher-led lessons and independent work time. Avoiding group work doesn't address the problem; it ignores it, which is hardly a solution. The real solution to reducing the threat that group work triggers is to make group work safe. Design group work so students have positive experiences and can grow to appreciate the benefits of learning from and with others without worry or fear.

Causes for students to view group work as emotionally, socially, or academically unsafe are likely to vary from student to student. Candid conversations about what they dislike (which could be code for "are threatened by") will lessen the guesswork on your part. If students are willing to share, then you can get started on designing interactions that consider their sense of safety.

You need to start small when students are skeptical about group work. Draw them in by easing their fears. Limit the time they interact, be explicit with how they engage, embed options to give them some control, and set them up to have a great time. Consider the source of worry and address it head-on.

Like most solutions in education, no single method works in all circumstances. I collected perspectives from students about why they avoid group work. Similar responses were combined and categories were chosen to represent reasons students dislike group work. The root causes for students to feel threatened by group work are shown in the first column of Image 1.2, along with strategies and comments to help create a sense of safety when working with others.

STRATEGIES WHEN STUDENTS ARE THREATENED BY GROUP WORK		
Root Cause	Strategy	Comments
They are introverted	Include individual time to think and process	As students prepare to engage in group interactions, allow individual students to gather their ideas and organize their thinking before they join the group. Then again after collaborating so they can process information on their own.
They lack social skills	Set norms for group work	How students agree, disagree, and interact are all important skills for collaboration, cooperation, and communication.
They don't see the value others can offer	Divvy up information to establish interdependence	Limit the information provided to all students by distributing portions of resources to different individuals. When another student has information everyone needs, their status is elevated and they have a meaningful contribution.
They do all the work anyway	Assign cognitive roles for each individual	Each student should have a role beyond housekeeping tasks that contributes to the learning. Group work is not intended to assess the knowledge of the collective group; it's designed to support each student's understanding.
They lack confidence in their knowledge	Pre-assess and provide positive feedback	Do a quick formative assessment or check for understanding prior to sending students into their groups. You may need to offer explicit affirmation for students unsure of themselves to help them build confidence.
They process slower than their peers	Pre-teach or expose some students to learning before others	Set students up for success by preparing them for learning that might be challenging or require additional processing time. Before sending them into groups, allow prep time to preview materials or organize their resources.
They do not feel accepted by peers.	Lay ground rules and explicitly teach soft skills	A foundation built on a positive culture is evident when students interact in groups. Classrooms that value individuals, practice empathy, and honor everyone will extend those behaviors into the partner or group time.

Image 1.2

WHAT YOU CAN DO TOMORROW

Creating a sense of safety is about setting the tone and building a culture where conversations and different views are appreciated and valued. Here are a few ideas for establishing an environment where student-to-student interactions are fun, helpful, and common in your classroom:

- **Standing conversations.** There is something about standing when we talk that makes the conversation feel more casual. Switch up the typical table talk and replace it with a standing conversation. You can keep the same nearby partners or invite students to speak to someone else in the room. This gives you a quick view of who is engaging and who is reluctant.

- **Allow students to choose their partners.** When a barrier to working in a group centers around friendships or relationships with peers, that problem can be reduced or completely eliminated by allowing them to select their partners. If you prefer not to offer this option to everyone, quietly ask a student who is resistant to group work who they would be most comfortable working with, and assign partners accordingly.

- **Add background music.** Playing music loosens people up a bit. When students arrive in class or interact during a student-to-student conversation, you can quickly liven up the room by playing upbeat music that is likely to be found on students' playlists.

- **Adopt accountability partners.** Classrooms where students monitor one another and hold each other accountable usually have productive group work. Accountability partners simply check in on progress. One teacher encouraged this arrangement by saying, "Set a goal with your accountability partner for how far you will get in the next seven minutes of work time." Then, after seven minutes, prompt students to report to their accountability partners to see if they fell short, met, or exceeded their goals. The accountability partners offer suggestions for focus, affirmation for a job well done, or praise for exceptional progress.

- **Pause for praise.** One of the most common worries students have when it comes to working with peers is how others perceive them. Positive interactions between students will help calm their fears. When you notice an opportunity to offer kudos to a student, invite other students to share the praise instead of you. Open the door to peers acknowledging and encouraging one another. These compliments or acts of gratitude go a long way toward making group work more inviting. The benefits hold true for both the person giving the positive remarks and the person receiving them. Win-win!

- **Start with partner activities.** As you ease into larger collaborative groups, starting with partners is a nice beginning step. Then use a strategy like `Pair-Square` to combine two partner groups into a single group of four. The advantage is that in their partner groups, students can build confidence and practice articulating their thinking. In the squared group, they are set up for success and prepared to listen for thinking that agrees, builds, or challenges the thoughts from their partner groups.

- **Ask for strategies.** Students might come to you with a combination of positive and negative experiences with group work. If they are unsure which outcome is likely in your classroom, they may be reluctant to engage. Ask them for strategies or protocols they have enjoyed in the past; it gives students a voice and just might add another tool to your toolbox.

- **Gamify activities.** When we play games, there are guidelines, rules, processes, and expectations for how to engage. All of these are helpful when working in cooperative groups. A trivia game can easily be flipped into assessing or reinforcing recent learning. Just swap out the questions the game provides for questions related to your unit and … presto! … you have a fun way for students to engage in content while interacting socially.

A BLUEPRINT FOR FULL IMPLEMENTATION

STEP 1: Establish norms for the classroom that carry over into group work.

Class contracts, norms, and agreements are all ways that teachers and their students can agree on how learning will occur and what they can expect from one another. As you and your class establish these agreements, include how students will apply expectations, such as how to handle conflict and maintain the dignity of others. Clarifying these expectations from the onset grounds them in the classroom's culture and easily transcends to when they interact in groups.

STEP 2: Choose protocols that are quick, interpersonal, and have a high likelihood of success.

At first, when you teach a new protocol, it's best to describe how it works and then give students a chance to walk through it when the stakes are low. Hack 4: Perform Dry Runs goes deeper into separating *how* students learn from *what* students learn. These protocols are quick and interactive, and they lend themselves to using high-interest topics to lower the pressure to share wise and thoughtful responses to content questions.

> **Turn and Ask**. Instead of launching kids to turn and talk to their partners, invite them to begin their dialogue with a question. When the first partner asks and the other responds, it provides the conditions for both partners to have an opportunity to share. Remember to offer some think time before they begin.

> **Conga Lines**. Put students into two lines or an inner and outer circle and have them face each other. Pose a question or prompt to everyone and allow the pairs to discuss the prompt for a short period. When time is up, one student moves down the line to find a new partner. In the new pairs, learners may

either summarize their previous conversation or engage in a new question or prompt.

Give One-Get One. Ask students to brainstorm ideas individually. Using a grid, students fill in as many boxes as they can with responses to the prompt. Then they are invited to approach classmates, give them an idea from their grid, and get one idea from a peer. Students continue to give and get until their grid is full.

Ask-Ask-Trade. Various questions are printed on cards and distributed to students. When time begins, students find a partner. The first partner asks the second partner to respond to the question. Next, the second partner does the same. After both learners have responded to the questions, they trade cards and find new partners and ask their new questions.

Fill Your Head. Students individually craft a response to a prompt. Then they roam the room sharing their responses and listening to the responses of others without writing them down. When their head is "full" of others' ideas, the student goes back to their seat and jots down what they heard. They continue to collect responses from others until time is up. Then, groups of two to four students compare all the information they gathered from others to come up with one synthesized response.

Stir the Class. Start students in groups of three. Assign a number to each student within the group. Provide the students with a discussion topic related to your lesson. After students have had sufficient time to discuss the topic, announce a number within their group. The student assigned to that number rotates to a new group and summarizes group one's thinking to group two. This person is now a member of group two. Pose another discussion item for groups to discuss and repeat the sequence, choosing a random student number to rotate.

I Have-Who Has? In this activity, each student is given a word to describe or define and a definition or description of another word. The first person begins by asking, "Who has …" then reading the definition or description provided on their card. The classmate who has the word that matches the definition or description speaks next by saying, "I have …" (insert word that was just described or defined), followed by, "Who has …" (read their definition or description). Change this up by varying the size of the group or the number of cards each student holds.

STEP 3: Gather student feedback.

After engaging in a peer learning activity, allow students to provide their thoughts on what they liked and didn't like or how it was productive or unproductive. This time should not be about what individual students did or didn't do. The goal of gathering feedback is to get student input on how they're feeling about the activity or group task.

If students provide positive feedback, probe a bit more to find out what specifically was the cause of success. When they articulate the cause to you, choose future learning structures that offer similar benefits. You'll find more information on reflection in Hack 11: Go Live.

When (not *if*) a protocol flops, it is even more important to debrief what went wrong. When you encourage students to voice their concerns, it validates their experience, gives you anecdotal data about the structure, and offers an opportunity for you to acknowledge and agree on whether the outcome met the goal. Communicating to students that next time will be different reinforces the message that 1) group work is not going away, and 2) next time will be a better experience.

OVERCOMING PUSHBACK

It's tempting to use student pushback as rationale for not implementing a method that will be a challenge. However, developing interpersonal skills and having time to engage in the content on various levels are critical parts of deep learning. Therefore, when we face concerns or pushback, it's necessary to address them in a way that sets up your class to overcome the barriers rather than allows them to prevent group work from happening at all.

We have too much curriculum to cover. This pushback could probably be copy-pasted into every Hack Learning book. It's true that the expectations for what students should learn each year in each subject are extensive. At the same time, school is not about covering curriculum or getting through units. It's about learning. In order for students to make connections to previous learning or life experiences, they must have time to interact cognitively with the content. Doing this with peers permits them to explore what they are beginning to understand, check their assumptions or connections, and engage in enough struggle that there is a higher likelihood that they will retain and retrieve their new learning in the future.

I have students with anxiety. Supporting students with anxiety is a reality in most classrooms today. Anxiety is heightened when students are worried or feel threatened about what *might* happen or what *could* happen. The mystery is reduced if students Perform Dry Runs (see Hack 4) or observe models of how group work will play out. Keep these students in the know by being clear upfront about what they can expect, and do not deviate. Students who suffer from anxiety will probably prefer to choose their partners. This also empowers them to avoid working with classmates who trigger discomfort. If you can't honor their choice for group members, it is usually possible to prevent them from working with people they'd like to stay away from. Soon after, address the conflict between them so their anti-pairing isn't permanent if it doesn't need to be. (For more guidance on teaching students with anxiety, read *Anxious: How to Advocate for Students with Anxiety, Because What If It Turns Out Right?* by Christine Ravesi-Weinstein.)

> ***Developing interpersonal skills and having time to engage in the content on various levels are critical parts of deep learning.***

I hated group work, so I don't want to force my students to do it. I shared a similar sentiment in the introduction of this book. Sometimes I loved group work, and other times I hated it. What that tells me is that there are conditions within collaborative learning that are more and less appealing. When a teacher can design group work to align with the more preferred conditions, there isn't a unilateral hate for working with others. You wouldn't say the same thing about reading or math. Why, then, do we entertain the notion that if students don't like it, we shouldn't bother to teach the skill?

Students are not always nice to each other. Learning how to get along with others, respectfully disagree, and honor one another are among the biggest benefits of group work. On the occasions when group members are not compassionate to each other, it's a signal that a mini-lesson is needed to focus on kindness, respect, or consideration. If students are rude or dismissive to one another, whole-group instruction isn't going to change the culture. It will only temporarily mask it. We are better humans when we learn how to interact with others who have different views, backgrounds, and experiences than ours. Group work furnishes an organic structure to apply positive character traits.

My content area doesn't lend itself to much group work. If you limit your thinking about group work to students reading and summarizing a text, then I can see why a physical education teacher or band director might argue that group work is not essential. However, when the definition is expanded to teamwork and harmony, we tell a different story. Wherever students end up in life, they will benefit from the skills they acquire when interacting with others. Hack 2: Talk the Walk is dedicated to elevating these critical communication and collaboration skills.

THE HACK IN ACTION

The amygdala is a major player for anxiety. People who suffer from anxiety live in a heightened sense of fear and stress for an unhealthy portion of their waking hours. To teachers and loved ones, it is hard to understand why some students make a big deal out of seemingly nothing. Why get worked up over who goes first if we know everyone will get a turn? These logical responses have no point of contact when the wise owl is not engaged. The sole job of the guard dog (amygdala) is to identify danger or threats. It doesn't have the capacity to problem-solve. It's not unusual for teachers and loved ones to wonder if students' anxiety will ever calm down. Onlookers who witness this physiological response usually don't see it coming, and they feel helpless.

I understand this all too well because my daughter, Allie, suffered from anxiety all through school. Thankfully, she had teachers who, even if they didn't understand the mental health struggles she faced, examined their hearts and dug into their nurturing instincts. Their efforts to create a feeling of safety for a young teen who wasn't safe from herself still impact Allie today.

The Hack in Action section of each chapter typically spotlights a single teacher. For this Hack, I'm highlighting multiple educators whose combined efforts built a strong, successful young woman who aspires to be a social worker one day—she feels called to do for others what amazing teachers did for her.

Here are some memories Allie Hamilton shared with me about times when a teacher made her feel safe:

- I knew he wasn't going to call on me when he gave me a quick little nod.

- She could sense when my anxiety was about to blow, sometimes before I did. She would ask me if I wanted to go in the hall and get a drink of water.

- She must have known my love language or something because she would just rub my back or tickle my arm. I hope teachers don't get in trouble for that these days.

- Somehow, she just knew when to give me space. How could she tell?

- The little room down the hall was open during lunch. I would go there, and she would tell me what we were going to read in class so I could read it first and not be embarrassed that I read so slowly.

- She treated me like a kid. Not a student. It made me feel like she was in my corner.

- The first time I had my menstrual period at school, you were away at a meeting. She took me to the staff bathroom and got a maxi pad, then she let me use that bathroom so nobody would see me walk down the hall with a pad in my hand.

- In that classroom, everybody acted differently. They were actually nice. Why couldn't they be like that all the time?

- When I came back to school after the hospital, she was the first person I wanted to see. Remember I asked you if she would be there?

- It probably wasn't true, but if I ever got in a fight, I think she would have had my back. Teachers probably don't fight though.

- She was so good at her job. That's the kind of social worker I want to be—only not in a school.

- I'm pretty sure I was her favorite. Teachers do have favorites, ya know?

- There were times when those boys were triggering me. He would stand between us so I couldn't see them. I used to think it was a coincidence. I bet he knew what he was doing.

- When we had to pick partners, she would call out, "Allie, you'll be my partner" before anybody even started to pair up. I was relieved because probably nobody would pick me.

- She told everybody that we were going to work in groups. I froze. Then she gave me a little smile, and I knew she picked good kids for me to work with.

- I was so embarrassed when I didn't know what a carnivore was. That was a rough night, remember Mom? After that, it was like he loved it when I asked questions. IDK why I wasn't embarrassed in that class anymore.

- It's like there was a forcefield around his classroom door and only happy things were allowed inside.

- She had a giant stress ball. It was blue. It worked.

- I actually think she saved my life. I should tell her that. No, I can't. I'd probably cry.

Let me pause and take off my author hat and replace it with my mom hat. As sure as you're reading this right now, someone's child is saying one of these things about you … and you don't even know it. On behalf of families everywhere, caring for students who suffer from active amygdalae, I want to say thank you. Just thank you, thank you, thank you.

When the brain (specifically the amygdala) senses potential danger, its defense mechanism kicks in. A person in fight, flight, freeze, or fawn mode relies on these automated responses, and the problem-solving center of the brain (the prefrontal cortex) goes into hibernation. Students who feel threatened by group work may have this reaction, even if the danger is not real.

Providing a sense of safety in group work settings allows learners to access the part of the brain that controls executive function, decision-making, and self-control. Without it, when a threat exists, emotions take over and learning and collaboration decrease substantially.

Calm the Amygdala Reflection Questions:

- Why is it a problem if students are threatened by group work?

- How does brain function apply to the Calm the Amygdala Hack?

- What are the steps for full implementation of the Calm the Amygdala Hack?

- How do you connect to the Hack in Action?

- How might the Calm the Amygdala Hack impact student learning?

Calm the Amygdala Application Questions:

- How does the Calm the Amygdala Hack align with your current instructional practice?

- How can you apply the concepts within the Calm the Amygdala Hack immediately?

- What might your students perceive as social, emotional, or academic threats in group work?

- What actions would help students feel safe during group work?

- How might Calming the Amygdala be used to benefit students with different needs?

- How will you monitor the impact of the Calm the Amygdala Hack on group work?

HACK 2

TALK THE WALK
Communicate Interpersonal Learning Targets

*Explain to me again: how come we treat reading
and mathematics as more important than
learning to get along with one another?*
— PENNIE BROWNLEE, AUTHOR, ADVOCATE,
AND EARLY CHILDHOOD EXPERT

THE PROBLEM: SCHOOLS DON'T EMPHASIZE SOFT SKILLS

EVERY TEACHER HAS heard, "When are we ever going to use this?" Heck, most of us probably wondered that ourselves as students, in meetings, or in poorly executed professional development days. Students who do not see the relevance in what they are learning are less likely to grasp new concepts, retain them, and transfer them to other situations.

Relevancy is a key component of making learning stick and activating intrinsic motivation to master a skill.

Academic learning targets are linked to content standards, unit objectives, and other learning goals. They provide clarity for students about the lesson's purpose. In an effort to maximize the benefits of group work, many lessons include peer interaction components to reach these content learning targets. Activities that include collaboration don't necessarily require that students work in a group. Oftentimes, it's possible that a task could be completed independently with each student engaging in the deliberate practice of a concept or skill. In those situations, we may foresee that some students would not recognize the added benefits of working with others and instead request to work alone.

For example, in one classroom I observed, students gathered in learning teams. Each group's purpose was to determine how authors use text structure to organize their writing. The activity was designed so each student contributed to the overall task. Even with interdependence and structured routines, students recognized that meeting the learning target didn't require them to work with others. Many requested to work alone. They didn't see the need to interact with peers. After all, although it would be a little more work, a single student could analyze multiple texts to determine text structure without a partner.

The teacher saw it differently. She designed the lesson to include trios of students working together. Her reasoning was that a few of the text structures were complex. She suspected that students would come to different conclusions about the text structure. Some would conclude that it was problem/solution, while others would argue that it was chronological. The dialogue in their groups would cause students to find textual evidence to defend their analysis and lead to the realization that some texts have more than one structure.

The teacher knew that the productive struggle and the argumentation would help students discover the complexity of the text on their own, even though she could have explained it to them. She shared the content expectation related to text structure but didn't share the interpersonal skills of listening to the reasoning of others and providing support for one's ideas. As a result, the learning target focused on text structure but was silent on the interpersonal skills that required group interaction to apply. It's no wonder that students didn't understand why they were asked to work together—they didn't know about the other goal related to soft skills.

Students who understand the learning target can have tunnel vision toward learning the specific goal for the day. Until now, you might have thought that was a good thing. And it is … except when another purpose goes unspoken, as in the case of interpersonal or soft skills.

If hard skills are *what* students are learning, soft skills are *how* they are learning. Hard skills focus on content in areas like math, social studies, music, reading, and art. In the working world, they are the abilities necessary for specific jobs. They are taught or learned on the job and can oftentimes be quantified or measured.

Soft skills include a variety of non-technical abilities needed to be successful in the workforce and in life. Employers in just about any field include soft skills like those listed in Image 2.1 as qualities they desire when hiring workers. This is by no means an exclusive list, but it offers plenty of examples to consider. Soft skills are often referred to as transferable skills because they are necessary for success in multiple industries. Some of these soft skills are personal traits, and others are more interpersonal relations. Read the list of soft skills through the lens of learner characteristics. How many of these attributes do we deem valuable for learners? Then review the list again and determine how many of them require interactions with peers in order to develop the attributes.

SOFT SKILLS

- Accepting Criticism
- Active Listening
- Adaptability
- Analysis
- Articulate
- Assertiveness
- Attention to Detail
- Brainstorming
- Collaboration
- Confidence
- Conflict Resolution
- Constructive Feedback
- Cooperation
- Coordination
- Cultural Intelligence
- Decision-Making
- Dependability
- Diplomacy

- Effective Communication
- Emotional Intelligence
- Empathy
- Encouraging
- Equitable
- Growth Mindset
- Idea Exchange
- Inclusivity
- Innovation
- Interpersonal Skills
- Leadership
- Mediation
- Mindful
- Negotiation
- Networking
- Non-Verbal Communication
- Open-Mindedness

- Optimism
- Organization
- Patience
- Persuasion
- Positivity
- Problem-Solving
- Reasoning
- Respectfulness
- Responsibility
- Self-Awareness
- Self-Management
- Self-Motivation
- Sociability
- Task Delegation
- Team-Building
- Teamwork
- Time Management
- Tolerance

Image 2.1

It will be a continuous struggle to encourage students to value interacting with peers if the purpose and the benefits are not called to their attention. Next time students groan about working with others or ask to work independently, before you quickly agree, pause to consider what interpersonal skills they will not be applying or practicing if they work alone.

THE HACK: TALK THE WALK

You know the cliché about when people say they are going to do something or speak about what should be done but don't follow through or abide by their own suggestions. These individuals are challenged to "walk the talk," meaning they should put action to their words. Another problem with group work is that students are expected to use soft skills, but these skills are rarely mentioned, let alone explicitly taught in school. We expect them to act but don't always communicate that expectation. In other words, we don't Talk the Walk.

Soft skills warrant the same intentional focus and attention as other goals like identifying text structure.

There's no need to keep the benefits of group work a secret. Consciously communicating the skills students should focus on helps them to intentionally practice skills and hones your focus and observation to a specific soft skill. When you Talk the Walk, you bring awareness to productive interactions that cross over into students becoming competent communicators and effective collaborators, and these interactions also serve as the method students use to deepen their understanding of the content. Review examples in Image 2.2 of how to Talk the Walk for some of the soft skills listed in the previous section.

TALK THE WALK		
Soft Skill	**Description**	**Value**
Articulate	Ability to communicate so others can easily understand.	Sharing your thoughts and ideas concisely causes your message to be received clearly.
Conflict Resolution	Solve problems with others peacefully.	Approaching disputes with calm and solution-based thinking reduces stress and tension in your group.
Empathy	Acknowledgment and understanding of others' feelings.	Considering and recognizing the feelings of others honors and respects them as human beings.
Inclusivity	Take action to welcome; include everyone.	Seeking all voices to be heard and valued leads to well-rounded thinking and inclusion.
Mindfulness	Awareness without judgment.	Noticing what is happening in the present provides opportunity to avoid conflict or shift situations when needed.
Questioning	Use of inquiry to clarify, deepen, or challenge ideas or understanding.	An inquisitive approach reduces misunderstandings, opens thinking, and explores doubt.

Image 2.2

Included in many state standards are speaking and listening skills that, when taught and used consistently, can be applied not only in any classroom but also beyond the school walls; they are skills used every day and everywhere. Through these standards, students develop soft skills and enrich their learning. Two categories are found in the speaking and listening strand of the ELA standards. The first is comprehension and collaboration. The second is presentation of knowledge and ideas.

Within these strands are goals for how students should interact with one another in ways that lead them to think critically, articulate clearly, engage in discourse, respond thoughtfully, promote divergent and creative perspectives, and propel conversations. These critical skills spelled out throughout our standards for learning are not extra, optional, or fluff. Soft skills warrant the same intentional focus and attention as other goals like identifying text structure.

WHAT YOU CAN DO TOMORROW

To Talk the Walk with soft skills, your students must understand why learning them is helpful, recognize when they need soft skills, and then execute them effectively. The following tips offer ways to call attention to soft skills and the value they bring to conversations and interactions with others.

- **Introduce the phrase "soft skills."** Explicitly share the words "soft skills" with students as a category for attributes people have and can develop to improve the way they learn or work. Moving forward, behaviors that show effective interactions, like adaptability or reasoning, can be easily identified as examples.

- **Label soft skills when they are applied naturally.** It's always helpful to be specific with your word choices. Rather than generalize effective teams as exhibiting "good group work," purposefully label the soft skills they used to achieve success. You might narrate that the constructive feedback they provided to one another was respectful and ultimately pushed them to achieve more success.

- **Connect soft skills to students.** Listen in on team discussions to observe soft skills individual students possess and apply. Maybe a team member noticed a peer was frowning as someone else spoke. Her invitation of "You look like you are confused or disagree … What are you thinking?" is a great example to demonstrate that a student is mindful and inclusive.

- **Identify undesirable interactions.** One way to increase the frequency of your references to soft skills is to connect events like "interrupting" to a soft skill that is needed, like "patience" or "self-management." Rather than prompt students to not interrupt, stamp the moment as an opportunity to execute the value of a soft skill like, "When you actively listen, you allow speakers to complete their thoughts."

- **Notice embedded soft skills.** Many times, curricular materials include soft skills that are emphasized or practiced during planned activities. As you review your lesson plans, notice when they are already placed in the lesson. That way, you have less planning to do (win-win!).

- **Announce an area of focus.** Before groups begin to work, inform them that you will be looking for evidence of how they are being equitable with talk time. Even if students only invite quieter students to share their thinking when you walk by, recognize it as evidence that students are mindfully applying soft skills in their groups. Members being aware of what their team needs is the first step to building productive groups.

A BLUEPRINT FOR FULL IMPLEMENTATION

STEP 1: Review your state standards to identify embedded soft skills.

There is a vertical alignment of thinking and collaboration skills within every state's standards. Identify those for the grade level you teach. They are included within many specific content areas and within the speaking and listening strand for ELA. If you're an art, geometry, or biology teacher, these soft skills expand into your content areas as well. Developing and applying these skills is not the sole responsibility of ELA teachers.

STEP 2: Observe students and take note of the skills they have and need to improve.

Once you have your list of soft skills, refer to it when you listen in on students' conversations and collaborative learning. Document where they have strengths and where they can benefit from applying the traits. Then take note of which skills are lacking. Maintain easy access to this list and visit it frequently. Use it to plan mini-lessons that target those skills or as reminders to apply them.

STEP 3: Communicate soft skill goals.

Whether you are introducing and explicitly teaching a soft skill that students need for quality conversations or you're expanding their use of a skill that they already know, disclose it to students. We only Talk the Walk when the methods for effective group interaction are clear to students. It's well worth the time it takes to communicate that their groups should focus on being encouraging and patient when their peers are sharing innovative ideas. The explicit reference to the soft skill will increase the likelihood that students will pause before interrupting and pose more clarifying questions when new ideas surface.

STEP 4: Co-construct success criteria.

Don't assume that students know how, when, and why to apply their group work skills. For example, when you focus on how to ask clarifying questions (more on questioning in Hack 10: Deepen Dialogue with Questions), be sure to teach how to ask for clarification, when it should be done, and why it improves group dynamics and communication. It's common for success criteria to be a checklist, rubric, or an "I can" statement.

When you're establishing what good questioning looks like, try modeling it. Set up a mock scenario so students can identify examples of ways to request clarity, such as, "Do you mean …" or "What does that acronym stand for?" Help students choose when to ask a question: Should they interrupt if the speaker uses a word they don't know or wait until the speaker pauses? Then role-play how groups interact with the benefit of questioning for clarity as well as the possible negative outcomes if the message remains cloudy. Through these co-construction exercises, group members will get a picture of what to do and what not to do.

Another idea comes from instructional coach Paula Warren. She shows her students videos of learning groups interacting. Some examples are highly effective, and others not so much. Mrs. Warren leads students through a critiquing exercise so they recognize specific ways that teams are experiencing success and honoring each group member. They also identify when actions could lead to unproductive groups or cause their peers to feel devalued.

Her students then apply the criteria to their own teams, even rating themselves against the students in the video.

STEP 5: Give equal focus to content and soft skills in group work.

With all this work and emphasis on the soft skills, it's important to carry it through. When you are monitoring the groups, pay attention to both the academic or content learning target and the soft skill learning target. Assess and provide feedback to individuals and groups around *how* they learn, not just *what* they learn.

OVERCOMING PUSHBACK

The amount of learning for any grade level or content area is tremendous. Including a focus on soft skills initially feels like you have even more to teach. Common concerns for Talk the Walk are spelled out here, along with considerations to ponder.

If I focus on soft skills, I won't have time for the "real" content. Soft skills are not fluff. We often expect students to use them but neglect to teach these skills. The point isn't to double your curriculum but to add value. It's ideal to determine what habits or soft skills students need, then communicate the soft skill goal when launching the activity.

Students have different cultural backgrounds. This is important to keep in mind. Not all students will interact with their peers in the same way. Some students might be more comfortable with close proximity, animated voices, or exaggerated physical gestures. We see those differences more clearly in a group work environment, and it helps us to appreciate and respect one another.

Establishing norms for the classroom from the onset provides the opportunity for students to express their preferences and agree on how they will communicate as they consider a variety of cultural backgrounds. Revisit these norms and cultural differences as needed. Eventually, as students become more familiar with one another, they will honor the preferences of one another and build their empathetic skills.

When you have students who lack understanding or face challenges with being open-minded and compassionate toward students who have different backgrounds or cultures, engage them in activities that allow them to learn about one another. If you are a teacher who identifies with the dominant culture or are not confident navigating difficult conversations, you may want to seek out advice or perspective from a director of equity or someone who can help you.

Kids should learn these skills at home. Even if I agreed that this is the sole responsibility of families (which I don't), if we desire to establish a safe environment where students feel free to take risks without threat of social ridicule or personal humiliation, then it's on us to consistently support positive interpersonal interactions. These are soft skills. It's not acceptable to expect behaviors yet be unwilling to help students develop them.

Determine what habits or soft skills students need, then communicate the soft skill goal when launching the activity.

What if I have special education students in my class with social goals on their IEPs? Great! By addressing soft skills, you will include the social skills that the IEP team agreed the student would learn. While these students might have a larger gap in their abilities to apply the skills they are learning, they also offer their peers an opportunity to practice acceptance, inclusion, patience, and empathy. This benefits everyone.

Soft skills are not on the report card or are not graded. Grading practices are irrelevant to the fact that soft skills are necessary for learning and life and need to be taught and fostered. To tackle the problems with grading practices related to soft skills or content goals, read *Hacking Assessment: 10 Ways to Go Gradeless in a Traditional Grades School (Second Edition)* by Starr Sackstein.

THE HACK IN ACTION

In my consultant role, I have the privilege of connecting with teachers all over North America. I've known many of them for years and have enjoyed watching them master the art of teaching. One such teacher is Paula Warren, who is currently an instructional coach in the Detroit area. She connected with Wendy Smith, an algebra teacher in the same high school, to brainstorm ways they could improve the quality of math collaborative groups.

The teachers found no trouble listing the ways students could engage more authentically and support each other to build perseverance when faced with challenging math problems. Until then, these high school students' exposure to group work in math class had been limited, but Mrs. Smith was determined to elevate the student talk.

Mrs. Warren suggested they step away from algebra learning targets and pause to co-create success criteria for effective conversations with the students.

They engaged in a modified version of **Affinity Mapping**, where students used sticky notes to brainstorm individually on this goal: *I am learning how to hold an effective conversation with my group in order to solve challenging algebraic equations.* Then, they came together in small groups and sorted their sticky notes into piles. They lumped similar descriptions together. Once all their sticky notes were clustered, they took one pile at a time and summarized it. Maintaining the essence of every sticky note was a must. When the group had a label for the pile, they moved on to the next pile until they had a short list of expectations that represented everyone's input.

To create a class list of criteria, each small group's shortlist was converted to sticky notes, and the process of sorting and combining went through another phase. Together, the entire class came to consensus on each of the descriptors, narrowing down the initial total of over one hundred descriptors to only nine.

They were:

- Building off of others

- One at a time

- Commit to the conversation (no phones)

- Respectfully challenging

- Make personal connections

- "Olive Garden volume" and speaking clearly

- Ask/invite others

- Opinions and explanations

- Engaged body language

The end result was an agreed-upon set of criteria that included every student's input. Students had rich conversations about what would enhance their group interactions in order to solve challenging math problems. Now Mrs. Smith can Talk the Walk with a list of interpersonal skills that create mindfulness and improve the quality of each group's interactions about math.

Elementary Adaptation: Affinity Mapping is a useful tool to organize and synthesize information without losing details. The added benefit of using this protocol for co-constructing success criteria is that when it comes time to get buy-in from the students, they are more willing because they identified what was important to them and what they perceived would be beneficial when they struggled with the math.

You can use the same process with minimal changes for younger students. If your classroom is self-contained, either keep the criteria broad enough to hold true for any time of day or describe what meeting the learning will look like by creating success criteria specific to reading, social studies, and other subjects.

Communication skills are necessary to articulate thinking, expand dialogue, and share meaning. To foster lifelong learners, children and adolescents must be empowered with *what* they are learning as well as *how* they are learning it. Not only are these skills vital in school, but also employers are intentionally seeking candidates who possess the ability to work with others.

Talk the Walk Reflection Questions:

- Why is it a problem when soft skills are not emphasized?
- How do the soft skills employers look for apply to the Talk the Walk Hack?
- What are the steps for full implementation of the Talk the Walk Hack?
- How do you connect to the Hack in Action?
- How might applying the Talk the Walk Hack impact student learning?

Talk the Walk Application Questions:

- How does the Talk the Walk Hack align with your current instructional practice?

- How can you apply the concepts within the Talk the Walk Hack immediately?

- What soft skills do your students already apply?

- How will you choose which soft skills to address when facilitating group work?

- How might the Talk the Walk Hack benefit students with different needs?

- How will you measure the effectiveness of soft skills in partner or group work?

HACK 3

CONVERT FOR INTROVERTS

Ease into Social Interactions

Without great solitude, no serious work is possible.
— PABLO PICASSO, ARTIST

THE PROBLEM: GROUP WORK FAVORS EXTROVERTS

PUT A BUNCH of teachers in a room, and we all have a different theory about why every year more kids prefer to work alone. Some say it's the two years they spent at home during the pandemic that began in 2020. Others blame technology and social media. Maybe there's something in the water that is causing more introverts to be born. Who knows?

By definition, group work involves working with others. The most effective groups are described as interactive, and they challenge one another's thinking. Some people live for this setting. They thrive on human interactions. These are the people who could talk for hours to a stranger at the grocery store. They feed off the stimulation of a lively environment. They look at public settings as opportunities to meet new people. They carry a deep joy for small talk and oftentimes verbalize their thoughts in real time. When a spontaneous moment occurs, they are typically all in and ready to go. Yep, these people are extroverts.

When considering how extroverts would perceive and interact in a group setting, it's a safe bet that they would be just fine. As a generalization, they probably prefer it. And if you were in the room with them, you would probably spot them easily because they are not far from the action. Learning that is designed for social interactions and external thinking that leans a little to the unpredictable side is custom-made for the textbook extrovert.

So if *extro*verts are people who are energized in social settings, that would suggest *intro*verts dislike social settings. People have defined introverts as shy, even antisocial. However, just because it's said doesn't mean it's true. It's not.

In fact, the assumptions that extroverts are confident and introverts are bashful are extremely inaccurate generalizations. What determines whether a person is more extroverted or more introverted is how they recharge. Introverts get their energy from within. They process their thoughts before sharing them. Small talk is often a challenge. They prefer close connections or one-on-one interactions instead of the big social events that their extrovert counterparts enjoy. Introverts generally avoid being the center of attention and are comfortable being in the background. If a change will occur, they likely prefer to be given time to prepare for the shift.

Classroom conditions that involve movement; the hum of a room full of chatter; and the physical proximity of other people, learning teams, and partner work make extroverts feel at home. More than that, they are drawn to social settings. That's because extroverts get their energy from being around people; the more the better. It's as if other humans are solar panels, energizing them with exuberance.

Conversely, introverts get their energy from within. The stimulation of a busy classroom requires them to expend energy as they absorb what's happening and begin to do what they do naturally—process internally. While many introverts can be friendly and open during a social event, afterward they often feel drained from so much activity and need to recharge. Sometimes they can find a convenient spot to be alone: a car, their home, even a bathroom—and it's enough to fire them back up so they're ready to go again.

Does this have you rethinking how you label introverts? Maybe you're an introvert and you didn't know it until right now.

Let's take all this information about introverts and extroverts and apply it to the students in our classrooms. Do our lessons favor students who thrive from being around people or those who need a moment of solitude? How many opportunities do extroverts have to energize? Do introverts have more or less of those opportunities? In a classroom of twenty-five or more people, how is time scheduled for introverts to process independently so they are prepared to interact with others?

The reality is that most classrooms favor extroverts and—instead of accommodating an introvert's genuine need for alone time—many of us pressure introverts to open up, relax, and have fun ... in other words, try to be something they're not.

THE HACK: CONVERT FOR INTROVERTS

One challenge with identifying introverts and extroverts is a matter of degrees. These personality traits do not have a yes/no answer, like whether you enjoy the taste of coffee. It's more of a continuum, like how much of a movie buff you are. Think of it as a scale where a level one represents the introvert who consistently prefers to work alone and rarely volunteers to contribute to a lesson publicly. A level ten is the student who goes out of their way to be the center of attention and socialize. Most people fall somewhere in the middle with tendencies to lean to one side or the other. Unfortunately, kids who are further down the introverted side of the scale experience uncomfortable situations every day of school.

From the onset of the school day, students are grouped together on buses, in cafeterias, and in busy hallways—all environments that cause introverts to expend energy to manage the hustle and bustle. Entering the classroom, introverts see desks or tables that require them to sit in close proximity to others, and they are often given little or no notice before they have to interact in social situations. The very design of learning provides opportunities for students to engage in collaboration, which is a key skill for effective communication. Therefore, social learning activities must be adapted to accommodate the needs of our quieter students. The solution, then, is to convert learning environments—not to convert introverts.

> **Each of us needs a balance of being able to stand and think on our own and also being open to new ideas we couldn't have developed alone.**

Relationships and connections to other people are important to humans. Cultures are considered individualistic or collectivistic. In collectivist cultures, group cohesion is prioritized over individual success. Individualist cultures value independence and freedom. Students who affiliate with either of these groups value connections to others. If you question the claim that students are drawn to interact with others, stop in the cafeteria or observe peer interactions in the hallways. Most often, students are eager to connect with others, and even those who are walking alone don't cringe if someone says hello or pays them a compliment.

Introverts value their relationships as much as extroverts. They just tend to have a tighter, more personal circle. All of this suggests that perhaps their desire to work alone is less about isolation and avoidance behavior and more about fulfilling needs like taking a break from the energy-sapping busyness and pausing to engage in a little introspection.

Each of us needs a balance of being able to stand and think on our own and also being open to new ideas we couldn't have developed alone.

When they are alone, introverts are in the zone. It's when they do their best thinking. Group work activities force introverts to gather ideas and process information in a way that is overwhelming, causes their work to suffer, and diminishes their learning.

Yet the converse is also true. In classrooms that have limited group work or student interactions, the learners who thrive by building on others' thinking are not given enough opportunities to learn in a way where they flourish.

The ideal classroom setting, then, provides balance for both types of learners.

Since most classrooms already favor extroverts, let's brainstorm how we can provide more balance to our group work and give introverts the best learning experience. Here are four tips to get you started:

Mix individual and group time. A structure that illustrates this is called One-Some-One. The name explains it pretty well, and Image 3.1 shows how that might play out in a group task. First, the three-step activity provides time for students to prepare before entering into groups. Second, they gather more information, organize ideas, or collaborate with their team. Third, they return to work on their own, using the experience in their group to enhance their own thinking.

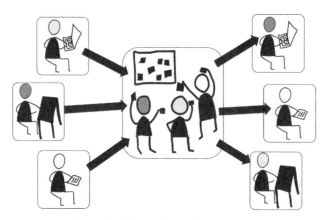

Image 3.1: The One-Some-One activity.

Build in quiet breaks. When tasks are energetic, there is a lot of movement, and the volume of the room is high, build in a quiet break. Inform students that until the timer goes off, they should work quietly or take a mental break. It doesn't have to be completely silent; a little focus music can help relax the vibe for a couple minutes.

Vary group sizes. When the task doesn't require exactly five people, offer for some students to work with partners. Introverts get the benefit of learning with others but also expend less energy keeping up with more people. Most often, it's okay to have different numbers of students in groups.

Design quiet zones. During collaborative learning times, there is bound to be talking going on. Take your introverts aside in advance and show them places in the classroom where noise doesn't carry as easily or where a bookshelf blocks the sound a little bit. Then allow them to have that preferential seating when appropriate.

An asset-based mindset helps us truly embrace the introverted personality. When we hold an asset-based perspective, we intentionally look for the benefits and strengths that exist in a scenario. Then we use those strengths to leverage and elevate others rather than focusing on deficiencies and working to fill them. An encouraging, positive growth mindset might sound like it's focusing on the good, but the target of the feedback is what the learning can *not* accomplish. Examples of deficit-yet-encouraging thinking stand next to asset-based thinking in Image 3.2, which I created for a book I co-authored, *Amplify Learner Voice* (get more info at hackinggroupwork.com).

Shift from Deficit Feedback	To Asset-Based Feedback
You'd rather work alone, but once you start working with your team, you'll have a lot of fun.	Your sense of humor is something that makes everyone on your team have fun. They're ready when you are.
I know it helps you to relax when you have some time alone. Go ahead and take a short break.	You're always ready to go when you get back from a break. We can jump right in when you get back.
You're going to need to study a little harder, but I know you can do it.	You can remember lyrics to so many songs, perhaps a jingle will help you remember this too.
If you don't have a quiet space at home to work, my classroom is always open every morning before school.	A quiet environment is something you said is helpful. My classroom is open every morning before school.
We all learn from failure. You just have to keep trying in class.	You never give up when you're playing that video game. Use that same perseverance to keep trying in class.

Image 3.2

We apply a deficit-yet-encouraging mindset when the subject of the feedback is negative. Asset-based feedback begins with the strength and elevates it to truly highlight the positive. When we try to change introverts by assuring them that they will be okay in their discomfort, we are sugar-coating the downside. Instead, we can find the sugar and sweeten our message through asset-based thinking.

WHAT YOU CAN DO TOMORROW

It's relatively easy to convert for introverts. Once you pause to consider these learners, accommodating lessons for them doesn't take much effort. The trick is to determine if an activity favors extroverts or introverts, then add or fine-tune in the lesson-planning phase instead of waiting until your introverts are uncomfortable and trying to adjust in the moment. Here are a few ideas to convert your lessons and group work activities to be more inviting and comfortable for students who are more introspective.

- **Inventory how you might group students.** Gather information and data about students that you could use to determine future partners or groups. This includes their interests, backgrounds, levels, personalities, working styles, friendships, introvert/extrovert tendencies, and more. You can use this information to create like-minded and diverse groups as needed with accommodations in mind for both introverts and extroverts.

- **Take note of how students interact.** When students choose their own partners, take note of how their conversations flow. Does one partner dominate the conversation? Do they lack listening skills? Are they using questions to deepen conversations? This will provide a baseline for the skills your students have and what they still need to develop. You can quickly gather multiple examples by using a strategy like Air Fives or Around the Clock.

- **Get outside.** In regions and times of the year when the weather is favorable, move the lesson outside. It allows students to get fresh air, builds in a little "me" time as you walk to your outdoor classroom space, and significantly reduces noise.

- **Give questions or task descriptions in advance.** Since introverts seem to prefer to think and process before they talk and interact with peers, provide questions or the expectations of a task before they move into groups. Everyone will benefit from the clarity of the activity. This allows time for introverts to familiarize themselves on their own before they are asked to engage. If you like, permit extroverts to bounce their thinking off a single partner before moving into the group. This design that includes both individual and partner thinking is a win-win when preparing for group work.

- **Put quiet kids near each other.** Students who talk less are often used as a buffer for students who chat or blurt. This might lessen the interruptions from your talkative students, but your quieter students are likely to feel a mismatch in their learning approaches. On the other hand, if you put two introverts next to each other, they will probably appreciate the fact that their partner isn't already talking the second you say "go."

A BLUEPRINT FOR FULL IMPLEMENTATION

STEP 1: Take your personal inventory.

Without thinking about it, we naturally make decisions about lessons based on what we prefer. If you know your working style and learning preferences align with introverts or extroverts, make sure you're not forgetting students who interact and learn in ways that are different than yours.

STEP 2: Fill your toolbox.

What are your go-to strategies? Analyze them for how they favor different types of learners and personalities. If you're short on strategies that embed individual think time *or* involve minimal interaction, search for new ones to add to your list. You can start with a few from this list (find full descriptions in the appendix and free resources at hackinggroupwork.com).

Chalk Talk. On a single sheet of large paper, have students brainstorm ideas based on a provided prompt or question. After sufficient think time, ask them to communicate only in writing on the chart paper. They can interact with the ideas but only in writing. They must stay silent. Provide each student with a different color marker so you can monitor the interactions between students to be sure everyone is equally represented.

Group Pick It-Show It. Groups of students have a single set of hold-up cards (ABCD, Agree/Disagree, or similar). Each time a prompt or question is shared, the partners or groups have to select a single response, and everyone must agree. The first team to respond with a correct answer gets a point.

Distance It-Show It. This is a modified version of group hold-ups. Instead of groups sitting near one another, they sit in their normal spots but away from their group members. Students have their own set of hold-up cards. When a prompt or question is given, team members hold up their personal responses. If their individual responses match their other team members' responses, everyone on the team gets a point, no matter how long it takes.

An additional option is to allow them to meet up if their answers are different to talk about it. You can play with the score by offering fewer points if the team needs to connect. This activity is especially effective if it occurs after groups interact and you're checking for individual learning as an outcome of the group working together.

Gallery Walks. After groups complete a project, students visit the other group stations. You can choose to have one of the group members stay behind to give a summary and answer questions.

Post-It Feedback. Bring in peer assessment of group products by having students visit the other groups and comment on their work. Arm them with two different colors of sticky notes: one color for Glows that represent compliments or strengths of a group's product and another color for Grows that offer suggestions for improvement or questions for the group to consider. Extend the task to give feedback on the feedback to make sure you aren't getting a bunch of "good jobs" that don't offer specific help.

Final Word. Highlight key points in a lesson and allow for multiple perspectives with this protocol. Each group member chooses three quotes from the text. Individually, the students reflect on their chosen quotes and prioritize them as one-two-three. The criteria for prioritizing can vary, such as key points, most resonating, and biggest "aha." First, students share their quotes without any explanation. The other students discuss the given quote while the first student listens. Set a timer for their dialogue. When the timer goes off, the first student shares why the quote was chosen and responds to the comments made by the other group members during their discussion. Repeat the process until every student in the group gets a final word.

Rinse and Repeat. This is intended to be short and sweet. Each student on a team takes a turn to quickly share comments about a lesson. No cross-talk is allowed, and students should be succinct in their shared thoughts. Use this to check for understanding and gauge learning within a lesson or as a lesson closure.

Back-to-Back and Face-to-Face. With a partner, students stand back-to-back so they cannot see their partner. Pose a question to the entire class and provide sufficient think time. During the think time, students remain with their backs facing their partners. When the signal is given (a direction or a sound), students turn around to face their partners and discuss the prompt. After a given time (45–90 seconds is often a good start), students return back-to-back in silence. Then the next prompt is provided. You may modify this protocol by switching partners between each question.

OVERCOMING PUSHBACK

Making modifications for every type of learning and differentiating for all student needs feels a little like working with the pieces of ten jigsaw puzzles in one box without a picture. Challenges are bound to surface. The results, however, are worth the effort. Let's look at a few of the most common concerns and how you can address them.

Convert your lesson structure to include opportunities for reflection, independent thinking, and individual planning.

It's my extroverts who cause the most problems. Actually, both student personalities can cause problems; it's just that one is more obvious than the other. Students who are unable to take a mental break and recharge are also posing a problem for student group work success. They're just quieter about it.

I think controlled chaos is good for learning. Many agree. This Hack isn't suggesting you hunker down and put your desks in rows to create silos. The goal is to strike a balance so one learning skill group isn't favored over another. All benefit from both learning environments.

Students will learn to interact with others at some point. That's my perspective as well. As they learn to interact with others, introverts will probably identify coping skills that help them prepare for those interactions by building themselves up in advance. Then they will need to learn to establish and maintain boundaries and develop ways to self-advocate. The solution isn't to change introverts into behaving like their counterparts. We can help our introverted students handle future interactions by finding ways to honor both types of learners and balance the learning activities. Again, everyone benefits.

I'm an introvert, too, so I like a more peaceful classroom. Your ability to notice that you are extending your personal preferences onto your entire class is an example of your professionalism and willingness to reflect. The goal isn't any different for teachers who are introverts. Balanced conditions that optimize the learning for all types of students are not only possible but optimal.

If I can't meet everyone's needs, why not just go with what-ever? We all have days when we want to throw our hands up in the air and ask a bunch of rhetorical questions. However, once your amygdala calms down, go back to the ideas in the What You Can Do Tomorrow section of this chapter. The tips may be easier than you expect without creating more work.

Isn't a quiet classroom a sign of teacher-centered learning? I suppose that if someone deems an active classroom student-cen-tered, then they might universally apply the opposite to a quiet room. The first incorrect aspect of that line of thinking is similiar to the misunderstanding about introverts. They are not the oppo-site of people who are social. Second, plenty of student-centered strategies and tasks are quiet. Third, to be blunt, I've been in active classrooms where there was no center of learning at all. The level of movement and the volume of voices are not the defining factors for who is at the center of learning.

THE HACK IN ACTION

Read this, and you'll never look at a purple folder in the same way again.

In a small resort community, there is a school system with only two buildings: an elementary school and a high school. It's the kind of town where everybody knows everybody. In the elemen-tary building, one of the classrooms had a student who was new to the area. Her newness itself wasn't noteworthy, but her unpre-dictable moods were. Since this young girl—I'll call her Joanna—was new, her teacher was still learning her backstory. She and the other teachers had some hunches based on their experiences with students who had been exposed to trauma, but they reserved their assumptions until they had more information.

Every day when the class gathered on the carpet, Joanna would clam up. I mean, she literally folded herself in half and buried her head in her lap. Sometimes she would command that the teacher leave her alone, but most of the time, she just stayed in her self-made shell and ignored everyone else. After a short time, she would open back up and join the class again. It wasn't terribly hard to manage, but when Joanna was about to clam up, she sent some signals that her classmates started to identify.

A few parents contacted the teacher, inquiring if anything was wrong with the new girl. The teacher assured them that the student was just fine. Since Joanna displayed signs when a clam-up was imminent, the teacher started to intervene. She would give Joanna attention, offer her special jobs, or engage her in learning by asking her to share her thinking with the class. None of the strategies could prevent the clam-up.

One day, when Joanna was inching away from her spot on the carpet, the teacher asked her if she would make an urgent delivery. She had an important purple folder that needed to go to the office. Joanna meekly nodded, took the folder to the office, and returned to her seat without a clam-up. Eventually, the purple folder became Joanna's daily hall pass. She walked it to the office, returned to class a couple minutes later, and had no clam-ups for an entire week.

Her teacher thought she would wean Joanna off the purple folder because Joanna seemed to be comfortable with the class by then. The first day they went without the purple folder, the clam-up returned. Finally, the teacher asked what happened when she took the purple folder to the office. Joanna said that the purple folder wasn't magic; she was missing herself. When she was with the other kids too long, she missed herself and that made her sad. The purple folder just allowed her to "be with myself," and that made her happy again. The two of them developed an agreement that instead of leaving the classroom with the purple folder, the teacher would make a special spot just for her to be with herself for two minutes.

I never heard that Joanna had overused the quiet corner. She was able to get some "me" time, recharge, and work her way back to the classroom. She self-managed and was part of her own solution. You can't ask for any more than that.

Teachers must consider many factors when planning for engaged learning with their lessons. How students process information and do their best thinking is a simple but critical detail of group work. Extroverts are generally comfortable and often look forward to the social aspect that collaboration offers. Introverts, on the other hand, are put at a disadvantage when they don't feel prepared to engage with others. Convert your lesson structure to include opportunities for reflection, independent thinking, and individual planning. Introverts are not antisocial or defiant. With some choice about space and partners and the time to focus inward before sharing outward, they are likely to increase their comfort level and set themselves up to successfully learn with and from their classmates.

Convert for Introverts Reflection Questions:

- Why is it a problem if group work favors extroverts?

- How does providing time for solitude contribute to the Convert for Introverts Hack?

- What are the steps for full implementation of the Convert for Introverts Hack?

- How do you connect to the Hack in Action?

- How might Convert for Introverts impact student learning?

Convert for Introverts Application Questions:

- How does the Convert for Introverts Hack align with your current instructional practice?

- How can you apply the concepts within the Convert for Introverts Hack immediately?

- What strategies do your introverts already have to recharge?

- How will you include students' choices and opinions when planning and applying learning routines?

- How might the Convert for Introverts Hack benefit students with different needs?

- How will you measure the impact group work has on introverts?

PERFORM DRY RUNS

Establish Protocols Before Content

*The shorter way to do many things is to
only do one thing at a time.*
— WOLFGANG AMADEUS MOZART, COMPOSER

THE PROBLEM: HOW AND WHAT TO LEARN ARE TAUGHT TOGETHER

WHEN TEACHERS INTRODUCE protocols or learning structures, students are often expected to learn the protocol and to process their learning about the content simultaneously. This divides their concentration between two concepts they are expected to learn, both of which we expect them to recall and apply in the future. For that to happen, the details about how to interact in a protocol *and* to understand the learning target must enter short-term memory, connect cognitively, then be stored for the long term. Learning a new protocol and new content at the same time causes the details to compete for the limited space in students' short-term memory.

Let's touch on a bit of neuroscience to truly understand why this is a problem. When we learn something new, we extend our brain power—or cognitive energy—to help our minds focus. Our brain holds that information in its short-term memory, which, in

71

the world of neuroscience, is sometimes referred to as working memory. This is where information is temporarily held, sometimes manipulated, and often forgotten because it doesn't make its way to long-term memory. Examples of when we use short-term memory but don't need the information to be stored in long-term memory include calculating a tip when paying your dinner bill, reading a recipe and remembering the ingredients and measurements as you bake, or putting an item in a spot to be retrieved later.

You can probably recall times when your mental math was interrupted and you had to start all over with your calculations instead of picking up where you mathematically left off. Or rereading a recipe three or four times to recall the amount of sugar needed for cookies, just to make sure you got it right. And, of course, we can all relate to the times when you can't remember where you put something but know you intentionally placed it somewhere for safekeeping. These are examples of when the details in your short-term memory are wiped clean and you cannot retrieve the information you put there a moment ago. You must either re-enter it into your short-term memory or use other strategies like retracing your steps to locate a missing item.

I like to think of short-term memory as a tool used to move a pile of dirt and spread it in a garden. Think of the learning students are engaged in as the dirt to be moved. The garden is their long-term memory. Some students have a small garden shovel to move the dirt. Other students have a wheelbarrow. The size of their tool determines how much dirt—or in this analogy, new learning—they can carry.

That's the first part of the problem: Students have different capacities for taking in new learning. If we try to overload the shovel or the wheelbarrow, dirt will simply overflow and not make it to the garden.

Next, as you transport dirt from your original pile to your garden, you might hit a rock in the ground or lose your balance.

Multiple events could cause you to lose some of your dirt along the way. Just because it fits on the shovel doesn't mean the dirt will stay there long enough to be spread in the garden. Metaphorically, what enters into the short-term memory (wheelbarrow) isn't guaranteed to land in the long-term memory (garden). That's the second part of the problem.

What does this garden have to do with teaching protocols and content? Everything. You see, protocols are one pile of dirt and content is another. When we want to move two piles of dirt at the same time, we have less room on our shovels or in our wheelbarrows for each. This is exactly what happens when we try to introduce a new protocol while teaching new information; something is bound to be left behind.

Unfortunately, this approach requires the student to decide which pile to tackle first. The result is a classroom of students who are at completely different stages in their gardens. Some will have moved one pile of dirt and learned the protocol; some will have tackled the second pile of dirt and interacted with the content. Inevitably, most will not fully succeed in either.

THE HACK: PERFORM DRY RUNS

Instead of introducing too much new information simultaneously, we can systematically fill the short-term memory, allow students to dump that learning into their long-term memory, then add more to the short-term memory. This process of creating bite-sized chunks of concepts, ideas, or knowledge increases the chance that students will be able to recall information in future lessons and in life. We do this by teaching protocols before content just as you would perform a dry run of a ceremony or theatrical show.

One benefit of using learning and talking protocols is that they provide a structure for how students think and interact with content, creating a thinking habit. The ability to know how to think and orchestrate their own learning is necessary to help students learn anything, not just today's lesson. While it takes time to teach the protocol, it really pays off throughout the year. It's just like teaching students how you expect them to enter the classroom. Once they learn the expectation, students know how to consistently find their spots and start their day.

> ## We can perform dry runs in classrooms to separate *how* students learn from *what* they learn.

The idea of practicing one part of a process before introducing the critical components is used in many settings. Actors run through their entire show without an audience and without stopping so that on opening night, everything goes smoothly. Platoons engaging in tactical training perform drills without live ammunition to eliminate the risk of danger. Legend has it that the term "dry run" originated when fire departments practiced responding to fires without using water.

We can perform dry runs in classrooms to separate *how* students learn from *what* they learn.

Conducting dry runs by introducing students to protocols saves you a great deal of time in the future. You reclaim the time you spent giving directions and explaining how you want students to engage when they have already performed dry runs. For example, teach students how to engage in a Triad, which is a three-person protocol that assigns roles as speaker, questioner, and summarizer (a list of protocols and more detailed descriptions can be found in the appendix). Students retain the understanding of how it works so that next time, you will not need to spend time addressing how they will listen, speak, and summarize what their peers are communicating in their groups. "We're going to use a `Triad` today" will trigger them to retrieve the process for engaging in a `Triad` just like the fire alarm sends firefighters to their engines. Consequently, you capture time you might have spent telling them how to learn and reallocate it for the actual learning.

When you want to use a new protocol, introduce it with low-stakes questions. These are questions that don't require students to think much about them, and there is little risk that emotions will come into play. Low-stakes questions interact with content that is familiar. It could be a perspective, an opinion, or knowledge that is quick for students to retrieve. The A^4 Matrix in Image 4.1 includes four quadrants to show the combinations of familiar and new protocols connected to familiar or new content.

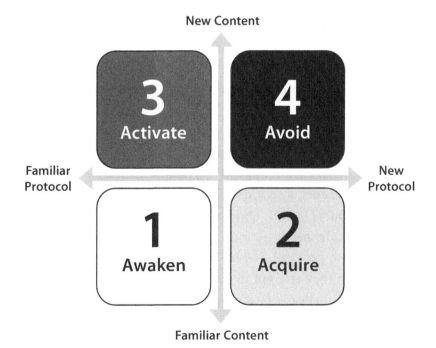

Image 4.1: An A^4 Matrix.

Use the quadrants to awaken thinking, acquire new protocols, activate new learning, and identify combinations to avoid.

Awaken, Quadrant 1: When both the protocol and the content are familiar, you can awaken student thinking to activate prior knowledge. For example, if your students have experience with a 2-Minute Jar, use it to recall the facts they learned about the solar system in previous grades. You're using a strategy and content that are both familiar.

Acquire, Quadrant 2: This is where the dry runs live. The content is familiar or low-stakes and is used to introduce, practice, and become comfortable with a new protocol. Suppose you are teaching students to use Through Their Eyes by asking them to take on the viewpoints of Mary, the principal, and the health department in the nursery rhyme *Mary Had a Little Lamb*. Since the activity is new but the nursery rhyme is familiar, it falls in the Acquire strategies quadrant.

Activate, Quadrant 3: Once a learning structure is familiar and little cognitive energy is necessary to execute it, you can use the protocol with new content. Let's take the same Through Their Eyes protocol that was taught with *Mary Had a Little Lamb*. Now that it's familiar, you can use this protocol to prompt students to see things from another viewpoint in the same way that toy makers, parents, and kids all think about a product from the lenses of producer, buyer, and consumer, respectively.

Avoid, Quadrant 4: Refrain from introducing new content through a new protocol. We risk students reaching information overload when they attempt to learn two distinctly different things simultaneously. Instead of expecting students to interact with Pinball Talk Moves while they are deciding on the most impactful character in the text, try taking a step back to Quadrant 2 and teach them to use Pinball Talk Moves as they discuss their opinions on the most talented musical artist alive today.

Target Quadrant 2 to Perform Dry Runs by asking low-stakes questions that don't take up room in short-term memory. When you do, all the available memory can be used for understanding how the protocol plays out. Going back to our gardening analogy, it is the equivalent of everyone starting on the same dirt pile so when the sun goes down, they have the same amounts of dirt (similar background information about the protocol) spread in their gardens. In the lessons that follow, your class can jump right into pile number two because the learning structure is already familiar. They can use their short-term memory to learn the new content you're teaching.

WHAT YOU CAN DO TOMORROW

You can take several actions right away to prepare you to Perform Dry Runs. These ideas will help you maximize the structure of the protocols you're using, and they don't require much effort at all.

- **Name your protocols.** It's hard to launch a protocol if it doesn't have a name. Think of the routines you have already established in your classroom and give them names. Instead of asking students to "Tell your elbow partner three things you are noticing so far," begin using the name of your protocol and say, "Use Turn and Ask to learn three things your elbow partner is noticing so far."

- **Get a sense of time.** Assigning a time frame to a task or activity creates a sense of urgency. It can be a little tricky, though. If you provide too much time, students can get off track or lag the next time you use the protocol. When you don't give enough time, students might wait it out and never even get started. So, before you jump into assigning fifteen seconds for thinking or two minutes for discussion, start timing how long these tasks tend to take. Using a stopwatch, begin timing how long portions of a protocol that you're already using take. Remember to count UP, not down. Check out Hack 6: Keep Time for more strategies.

- **Assign clock partners.** To help you quickly pair up students, assign them multiple partners and set "appointment" times. Some teachers intentionally connect students based on their academic levels, interests, backgrounds, or personalities. For example, when students meet with their noon partner, it might be someone at a similar reading level allowing for ease in differentiation. Alternately, the three o'clock partners might be students with similar backgrounds so they can leverage common experiences as they interact with learning.

- **Teach strategies you want to use later.** It's never too soon to introduce protocols or learning routines to students. If you notice that students in groups are struggling to slow down and check assumptions, Red, Yellow, Green Light is a perfect strategy. Introduce the language of red to stop and question what's being shared, yellow to slow down and wonder or make connections, and green to affirm that understanding is clear.

- **Anchor your classroom.** Look around your room and determine where students could meet up or connect with their peers. Then label those areas so you can direct them to move quickly. Some teachers use Four Corners and label them A, B, C, and D. Others might have space along classroom walls designated as north, east, south, and west walls. In the secondary level, a general area that pulls kids out of their seats and encourages them to mingle and talk could be named "the gathering area." Many lower elementary classrooms have a "carpet" spot where students meet for instruction. Once you have anchored areas within the classroom with a label, students know exactly where to go if you say, "If you think this, head to the east wall. Those of you thinking that, make your way to the south wall."

- **Collect engaging questions.** When you introduce new protocols, you need to have low-stakes questions ready. Begin gathering silly, fun, or simple questions you can use to walk students through a new learning routine. If the protocol requires more than a simple response, you can always add "why" or "explain your answer" to trigger additional details and conversations. In Image 4.2, you will find a few categories to get you started.

Low-Risk Question Category	Sample
Ask content questions they are sure to know.	How many things can you name that start with the letter B?
Revisit classroom norms or routines that are already established.	How do we know when class is over?
Ask questions about their interests.	What do you do for fun?
Explore some of their experiences.	When did you laugh so hard you almost cried?
Give choices with "Would you rather?"	Would you rather be in a room filled with spiders or snakes?
Inquire about preferences.	Is a rainbow or a sunset prettier?
Wonder about silly things.	What would be different if you were the principal?
Pose "what ifs."	If you were an animal, what kind would you be?

Image 4.2: Low-risk question categories.

- **Offer students choices on how they engage in a specific group activity.** As you build a toolbox of different protocols, you will collect a growing number of choices. To help draw attention to the protocol and trigger student reflection on how learning routines support their thinking, do a quick Standing Poll so students can offer their input. For example, "Stand now if you think Ask-Ask-Trade is the best way for us to share our thinking," then repeat the poll for a different protocol choice. Whatever has the most students on their feet will be the routine they use.

A BLUEPRINT FOR FULL IMPLEMENTATION

STEP 1: Identify protocols you can use throughout the year.

Ideally, some protocols are taught at the beginning of the school year so you can access them all year long. However, anytime is a good time to bring in a new structure for students to engage in thinking or talking. Different protocols serve different purposes, so as you gather a handful, be sure to include some that allow students to brainstorm, process information, give everyone a voice, engage in discourse, come to agreements, or summarize their group's thinking. The list of protocols in Image 4.3 provides examples and options for you to check out. If you have tried-and-true protocols or learning routines, determine their best use and add them to these categories. Descriptions of all the protocols shared in this book can be found in the appendix.

Brainstorming	Process Information	Everyone Has a Voice
• Brain Dump	• Reciprocal Teaching	• Triad
• Chalk Talk	• 3-2-1	• Back-to-Back
• See-Think-Wonder	• Shared Note Taking	• Conga Line
• Give One - Get One	• 3-Step Jigsaw	• Ask-Ask-Trade
Engage in Discourse	**Come to Agreement**	**Summarize**
• Final Word	• Spend a Buck	• KWL Chart
• Sentence Stems	• Finger Votes	• 6-Word Summary
• Fan and Pick	• Silent Choice	• Rinse and Repeat
• Word-Phrase-Sentence	• One Up Prioritizing	• Make an Analogy

Image 4.3: Categories for some of the protocols.

STEP 2: Establish a schedule for introducing the protocols.

After you introduce a protocol, you will want students to practice it until it feels familiar. Once they can apply the steps of the protocol without much thought or effort, you're ready to add content. It will work best if there isn't much time between when you teach a new learning routine and students practice it, and when they are asked to use it with learning targets.

Some protocols like Choral Response, which prompts all students to share a short response in unison, can be taught, practiced once or twice, then used immediately with content-specific questions and responses. Other protocols that are complex or time-consuming require more purpose and planning before being introduced. If you anticipate that students will need five or ten minutes to work through the steps of a protocol, you will need to include that time as you plan your lesson. You may choose to teach the protocol the day before rather than use time the day of the lesson.

> **Anytime is a good time to bring in a new structure for students to engage in thinking or talking.**

In elementary classrooms where students stay with the same teacher for most of the day, a protocol can be taught and applied during a morning meeting then used in the afternoon for a science or social studies lesson. At the secondary level, teachers don't have that same flexibility, so the decision is based on how much time is available within specific lessons. If you know an activity will be completed before the end of the hour, consider using the rest of that class period on Monday to teach a protocol you plan to use on Thursday.

When you typically dedicate some of your class time—at the beginning of the year or term—to share housekeeping information or get to know your students, this is the perfect time to include strategies that you can add to your familiar protocol list, allowing you to access them whenever they fit. Like anything, if too much time goes by between when you teach a protocol and when you apply it, a quick refresher might be helpful.

STEP 3: Prepare low-risk questions.

This is the step that determines where you fall in your A^4 Matrix. Since you are starting at Quadrant 2, where protocols are first taught, you need a handful of questions or talk prompts that do not emphasize the question or prompt. It doesn't matter if students like ice cream more than cookies, but if you want students to improve their listening skills, asking their preference provides an opportunity to practice listening and paraphrasing when engaged in a talk protocol. Be sure to revisit Image 4.2 for inspiration.

STEP 4: Introduce the routine.

Depending on how complex the routine is, determine if you will introduce all the steps at once or one part of the protocol at a time. One Word is a protocol where students share one word from the text for their team members to discuss, and it can likely be described in its entirety. However, Stir the Class, a protocol that involves groups of three students discussing a prompt, then one student moving to another group to offer a summary, is better to walk through one step at a time.

Remember to name the protocol and repeat the name of it as students are interacting. You can't over-say it. If students begin to comment on how often you're saying Brain Dump, then you're doing great.

STEP 5: Assess and reflect.

When students have executed the protocol with success and some level of consistency, then you are almost ready to add content and move to Quadrant 3 of the A^4 Matrix. The goal is for the protocol to make thinking and learning smooth, structured, and more productive. Therefore, students should automatically engage in the protocol. After each run-through of the protocol, invite students to reflect on its effectiveness.

Try these reflective prompts to solicit student input about the protocol itself:

- How is this protocol helpful?

- How was the timing of each step?

- What part did you most often forget or have to try again?

- What challenges emerged?

- What modifications could be made to improve its effectiveness?

- What communication skills were needed?

- How is this similar to or different from other routines we have used?

- When would this protocol work best?

- How do we know if we are ready to use this with our learning target today?

When students provide their feedback about the protocol, allow both their positive and negative comments and include them when appropriate. Your students' focus on the protocol and how to make it productive is triggered more with a question than a solution. For example, if they share that their group kept forgetting to trade papers, inquire with, "What might help you remember to trade papers?" instead of "Make sure you pay attention to step three that tells you to trade papers."

STEP 6: Execute the protocol with new content.

Once students have a handle on how to interact with the protocol, you're ready to use it with new learning. This moves you to Quadrant 3 of the A^4 Matrix. Do not let too much time go by before you get to this step. If the protocol is simple, you might even be able to apply it in the same lesson. More complex protocols can be taught on day one with the content added on day two. That way, you can take advantage of your class's recent mastery of the protocol with low-risk questions.

OVERCOMING PUSHBACK

Here are concerns that might surface as you consider how to implement the Perform Dry Runs Hack as well as solutions for handling them.

It will take too long to teach protocols. It does initially require a bigger time commitment to frontload protocols. Happily, you will gain that time back (and then some) throughout a unit or school year in the reduction of time needed to provide directions. When students know the general steps for Fan and Pick, a protocol that rotates a placemat to assign questioners, responders, and feedback givers, it's no longer necessary to explain how to place the mat.

Students don't follow directions. If you find that students are having trouble executing the protocol, there could be a variety of reasons. Here are two. It's possible there are too many steps shared at one time. In that case, either walk students through the protocol piece-by-piece or display all the steps in the routine. Another reason that students might drift from the directions is that they are too focused on the content. If that happens, revisit the protocol with even lower-risk questions.

Not every student will remember the protocol for next time anyway. That's the beauty of group work. It doesn't matter if *every* student remembers the entire protocol. We only need one student per group who has a handle on it. Then you can position them as leaders to describe and trigger their teammates' memories. If it's been a while since you last used a particular protocol, it's a great idea to give students a moment to recall what they do remember about it then team up to fill in the blanks.

When low-risk questions are about the students, some kids don't want to share personal information. This is an important detail to consider. Stay away from questions that assume students have had the same life experiences that may trigger anxieties. This is especially true at the beginning of the school year when you're getting to know your students. Later in the school year, when you are more familiar with your students, you can better anticipate what might be uncomfortable for some. For example, if a student's dog recently ran away, it would be a good idea to stay away from prompts about pets when you are teaching the new protocol.

THE HACK IN ACTION

A middle school art teacher was building her students' critiquing skills. Before this lesson, the primary criteria students used were their personal preferences to say whether they liked a piece of art or not. She wanted them to dig deeper. She tried to have them critique in partners in hopes that they would find a feature or element to explain why one piece was better than another in their eyes. However, their justifications were often shallow and felt more like afterthoughts.

Then she decided to try a strategy I had used in a workshop she attended. It was called Spend a Buck. She questioned if her students would be able to critique a piece of art based on interpretation, so she started small.

She asked students to think of their favorite snacks and list them. After they created their lists, they had to choose four entries from their lists: the first item they wrote down, the last item they wrote down, and any two in between. Next, students were given an imaginary dollar. They had to allocate their dollar between the four snacks. Every snack had to get some money, and no two snacks could have the same amount. The best snack should get the most money, and so on.

Her students had fun but still took the task seriously. Then she repeated the task, but this time, they had to work with a partner and the two of them had to spend their buck together. Students were getting the hang of it, and the math teacher down the hall loved that students were connecting decimals, ratios, and percentages in another class. The next time they attended art class, the students asked to Spend a Buck again. She agreed.

This time, she swapped the snacks for pieces of art. Students had to spend their money based on what piece was the strongest example of symbolism. Students discussed with their partners and made solid arguments for why the symbolism in one was better than in another. The students used Spend a Buck to critique art for the rest of the year. She changed the artwork based on the styles they were studying as well as the criteria. The class started with symbolism then moved on to descriptive backgrounds, the ability to portray a mood, and more.

The teacher performed a Dry Run with students so they could grasp the concept of ranking and prioritizing quality or value. Once they were hooked on the fun of making their arguments and spending their funny money, she brought in the art!

Elementary adaptation: Students who haven't yet grasped the concept of money or the value of a dollar can "spend" a pile of bingo chips, Unifix Cubes, or other tangible objects. For example, "The sentence that summarizes the text in the best way gets the most cubes. Every sentence has to get at least one, and no two sentences can receive the same number of cubes." Sound familiar? Same parameters, different "money." The Spend a Buck strategy can be used to prioritize or evaluate just about anything.

Dedicating time and attention to teaching new protocols before introducing new content provides learners with a chance to concentrate on the method they will use to engage in thinking, talking, and understanding the content. Once they master a protocol, students no longer use mental energy to think about the steps of the learning process. Instead, the process becomes the vehicle for learning. The protocol serves as a guide for how students interact with the content. Using protocols repeatedly reduces the time needed to provide directions and embeds familiarity within the lesson so students can focus on thinking in complex ways.

Perform Dry Runs Reflection Questions:

- Why is it a problem to introduce a new protocol while teaching new content?

- How does the A^4 Matrix support the Perform Dry Runs Hack?

- What are the steps for full implementation of the Perform Dry Runs Hack?

- How do you connect to the Hack in Action?

- How might applying Perform Dry Runs impact student learning?

Perform Dry Runs Application Questions:

- How does Perform Dry Runs align with your current instructional practice?

- How can you apply the concepts within Perform Dry Runs immediately?

- What protocols have your students already mastered?

- How will you gather low-risk questions to use when teaching new protocols?

- How will you include students' choices and opinions when planning and applying new learning routines?

- How might Performing Dry Runs benefit students with different needs?

HACK 5

ADD AN "I" TO TEAM
Encourage Self-Awareness

Individual commitment to a group effort—
that is what makes a team work, a company
work, a society work, a civilization work.
— VINCE LOMBARDI, AMERICAN FOOTBALL COACH

THE PROBLEM: OWNERSHIP OF RESPONSIBILITY IS MISSING

VICTORIOUS ATHLETIC TEAMS around the world often credit their ability to work as a unit for achieving success. Many even proclaim the common mantra that there is no "I" in TEAM. Yet if we hope to inspire students to work collaboratively, this mindset is missing a crucial message: If there's no I in TEAM, then who's responsible for me?

The prevalent problem of students not holding themselves accountable for their contributions, their learning, or the group's success surfaces in many ways. When facilitating group work, teachers everywhere share the following frustrations that often cause them to avoid this method of collaborative learning:

- Learners are unaware of their impact on the team.

- Students do not contribute to the group.

- Team members argue and are unproductive.

- Conflict is not addressed or resolved.

- Tasks are delegated unequally.

- Frustration causes kids to give up.

- Group members believe students who require additional time or other support don't add value.

- Individuals blame each other for group problems.

- Confusion is not resolved.

- Focus is on finishing instead of learning.

- Collaboration is diminished to working individually at the same table.

Admittedly, even adult committees, teams, and groups struggle with working together. Countless books are designed to help organizations establish a more collaborative atmosphere. Personality conflicts, poor social skills, and a lack of goal and task clarity contribute to wasted time and meetings that accomplish very little. This is why employers require qualifications that include excellent communication skills, the ability to work with a team, and self-motivation from potential job candidates.

Can you recall a time when you were on a team or worked with a partner and you really clicked? What made that group successful? View the descriptors in Image 5.1 that are commonly used to describe effective teams. How many align with the team or partner you are thinking about? If attributes that come to your mind aren't on the list, feel free to add them.

Accepting	Efficacious	Fun	Purposeful
Adaptive	Efficient	Helpful	Relevant
Beneficial	Empowering	Honest	Respectful
Challenging	Encouraging	Honoring	Resourceful
Comfortable	Energetic	Inspired	Rewarding
Committed	Engaging	Knowledgeable	Safe
Creative	Enlightening	Motivating	Skilled
Curious	Equal	Open	Strategic
Dedicated	Equitable	Organized	Supportive
Dependable	Explorative	Perseverant	Thoughtful
Diligent	Fair	Personable	Useful
Diverse	Flexible	Positive	Valued
Effective	Friendly	Productive	Welcoming

Image 5.1: Descriptors of effective groups.

Next, review the descriptors you identified and ask yourself if you displayed these traits. Educators are too modest; it's not conceited to recognize your positive attributes. Be honest about the contributions you brought to the team. If you're like most, you align with many of the characteristics you used to describe the whole group. Sure, some members of your team might have been more energetic than others or have more knowledge of a particular topic. However, quality groups are made up of quality individuals.

So, where did you learn to be dependable? Open? Encouraging? Chances are, you credit experiences in your life that exposed you to positive traits, you valued them, and then you sought to adopt those same approaches when interacting with other people. Students will develop these invaluable life skills if they also have experiences where they can feel the power of being respected, witness the outcomes of curiosity, and come to appreciate thorough organization. It's our job to provide these opportunities.

Although companies appreciate and value these soft skills, they rarely provide the training to develop them. The same happens in schools. Learners are expected to engage in collaborative, cooperative learning, and we notice when these skills are not present. Yet, learning targets that intentionally and explicitly teach positive interpersonal relations are hard to find. Students can't hold themselves accountable for skills they don't have yet. As a result, groups consisting of students who are unprepared to collaborate will not be collaborative.

Students will develop these invaluable life skills if they also have experiences where they can feel the power of being respected, witness the outcomes of curiosity, and come to appreciate thorough organization.

THE HACK: ADD AN "I" TO TEAM

Productive groups require a set of skills that every member must possess. Different personalities and life experiences create a continuum of how well individuals execute these skills. And, if you believe in a growth mindset, you ascribe to the notion that collaboration can be taught and improved. These are valid points.

However, the idea that there is no "I" in TEAM suggests that individuals have no accountability, impact, or contribution to a group's success or failure. Businessman and former professional basketball player Michael Jordan does not embrace that message and often retorts, "There is no 'I' in TEAM, but there is in WIN." Coming from a man who has an impressive number of wins, it is obvious that we need to add an "I" to TEAM.

Imagine the magic of students holding themselves accountable for their own learning and their group's success. These empowered learners would take the initiative, be focused on the learning goal, appreciate the contribution of others, and hold the culture of the group to a high standard that maintains everyone's dignity throughout the process. Sounds like rainbows and unicorns, right? It really isn't. It does, however, require you to cultivate an environment where honoring every person and celebrating the learning journey is at the core of your teaching.

Adding an "I" to TEAM means including a layer of self-awareness to each aspect of the team's interactions. Image 5.2 (available as a free download at hackinggroupwork.com) illustrates how I-TEAM is described:

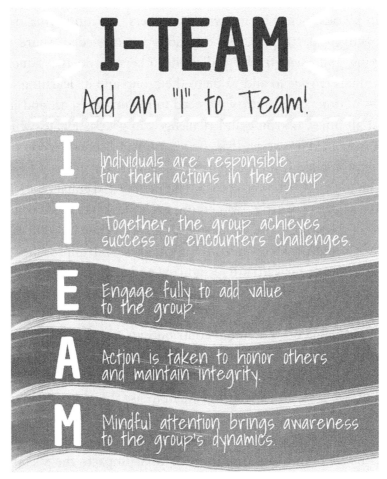

Image 5.2: The I-TEAM poster.

I – Individual. Starting with "I" calls attention to the truth that *individuals* are responsible for their words and actions. Regardless of what happens within the group, each individual owns how they react or respond to conflict. They recognize that they have an impact on how the group interacts and ultimately what is learned.

T – Together. The "T" reminds students that each individual's function is to move the entire team to success. Success is achieved as a group when every person on the team reaches the group's goals. Thus, individuals strive to learn *together*.

E – Engage. For "E," we note that individuals contribute to the group by advancing their own and others' learning. This means they actively participate, ask questions when needed, share their thinking and ideas freely, and invite others to do the same. So, individuals *engage* to add value to the group and its learning.

A – Action. "A" identifies the need to maintain respect and integrity at all times. Learning and challenge can get passionate, which is often welcomed. However, that passion cannot dishonor group members or prohibit learning for any group member. Therefore, individuals commit to taking *action* to protect their dignity and enhance learning.

M – Mindful. Lastly, "M" emphasizes the importance of being aware of the group's dynamics and progress. When a problem surfaces, it's addressed respectfully. Strategies and approaches that move the group forward are recognized and celebrated. When individuals are *mindful*, they notice the climate of the group and maintain a positive group experience.

Placing value on individual contributions to the group does not indicate that a single person is more important than another or even the whole group. The purpose is to enlighten students to the impact they have and encourage them to use it in ways that benefit everyone. That requires them to think about what they can accomplish together, to be actively engaged in learning, to take action when needed, and to be mindful of what impacts the social and academic progress of the group.

WHAT YOU CAN DO TOMORROW

Adding an "I" to TEAM is a continuous effort. Nearly everyone on the planet could stand to sharpen their I-TEAM skills. Fortunately, there are some actions you can take right away that will move your students toward holding themselves accountable for the successes and challenges their group faces.

- **Shift the focus between what they are learning and the thinking behind it.** Periodically stimulate metacognition (thinking about thinking). Growing as a learner means that skills and strategies to learn *anything* are developed over time with practice. While the content is important, how students are interacting, engaging, and understanding that content is a transferable skill that they will apply every time they encounter a new learning opportunity. To accomplish this level of metacognition, students must pay attention to the thinking they are using as they learn. When you call attention to how students are learning, whether it's annotating a text or making models, you highlight the learning habits that lead to success.

- **Play team games.** To emphasize the fact that groups succeed and face problems together, engage students in games that have a team mode, like Kahoot! or Quizlet Live (both online).

- **Use concise language when sharing emotions.** When dealing with various personalities and groups, there are bound to be conflicts from time to time. Normalizing the fact that humans feel different emotions at different times provides your students with an environment of emotional safety. The freedom to voice emotions communicates that students are to be heard and honored. Specific descriptors for emotions provide more accurate explanations for how a student is feeling. For example, a student might say they're angry because they weren't allowed to explain their idea. A more precise word might be devalued, unappreciated, or dismissed. There is a difference between angry and unappreciated. How groups rectify a problem and prevent members from feeling that way again is the difference between making them happy and showing respect.

- **Include cause-and-effect language in social settings.** Children who are still developing their social skills don't always see the direct link between their choices and how they impact others. As this ability to be mindful and empathetic evolves, explicitly label the connection. For example, "When you return the supplies to the cabinet where they belong, it allows others to access the supplies, too." Another example: "When you wait before blurting out answers, it allows everyone to have time to think."

- **Engage students in team-building activities.** A quick Google search for "team-building activities in school" will give you more than enough ideas for how to produce the conditions for students to practice working together as a unit. Reflecting on these tasks illustrates the "T" part of I-TEAM and demonstrates that successes and challenges are experienced by the entire group.

- **Label actions that support learning.** Assigning language to steps students take to help themselves and others learn permits you and your students to revisit that action. Naming strategies allows these actions to be stored and recalled for future use. When a hack works, label it or ask students to give it a title. Then when they're stuck on a similar problem down the road, they might remember that Blinky Blink resets what they're seeing and gives them another look with fresh eyes.

- **Practice empathy.** We need a lot more empathy in the world. Period. When it comes to helping students add an "I" to TEAM, empathy keeps a focus on honoring everyone in the group and acknowledging the value of each classmate.

A BLUEPRINT FOR FULL IMPLEMENTATION

STEP 1: Introduce I-TEAM.

The I-TEAM represents how individuals in a group consistently focus on their own contributions to the collective success of the team. A system will not function properly if one of its parts isn't working. An ideal way to illustrate this is by using a Rube Goldberg machine. The game *Mousetrap* and countless YouTube videos can serve as a model. My personal favorite is a YouTube video called *Audri's Rube Goldberg Monster Trap*.

Any Rube Goldberg machine makes the point that each individual component must do its part to execute the final task. If the machine breaks down, it can be modified and tried again and again until all the parts are working in unison. Each piece is critical yet no more or no less important than another. While there is accountability for each component, none of them work alone.

This is the mindset we want to have in our learning groups.

STEP 2: Build togetherness.

The second descriptor in I-TEAM is togetherness. Engage students in activities that require them to work together to accomplish a common goal. Try some of these ideas:

- **Classroom escape rooms:** Find free examples of classroom escape rooms and have your teams complete the puzzles to "escape." Because the purpose is to build teamwork and togetherness, make sure every group makes it to the end. If you want to build your own, websites like We Are Teachers offer step-by-step directions for customizing your activities.

- **Build it:** Encourage creativity and critical thinking by tasking groups to work together and build something with limited materials. For example:
  - ▶ Design a bridge with straws that will hold a toy car.
  - ▶ Build a tower with twenty sticks of raw spaghetti, one yard of tape, one yard of string, and a large marshmallow.
  - ▶ Create a way to protect an egg when dropped from a specified height. Provide several options for materials such as paper, Styrofoam packing materials, toothpicks, and plastic straws.

- **I See-You Draw**: Situate students so they are facing in opposite directions. Give one student an image or random shape and the other student a piece of paper and a pencil. Neither partner can see the other. The student with the picture describes it to their partner, who then attempts to replicate the image using only the verbal descriptions provided. Emphasize the power of questions by not allowing the drawer to ask questions the first time but allowing them in the second round with a new image.

- **Icon Story**: Group members tell a collective story, one person at a time, using a stack of preprinted random images on cards (such as a train, shoes, flag, and volcano). One person begins the story using an image from the pile as inspiration. As the story progresses, team members must intertwine their images into the group's story. For added fun, allow each group to retell their icon stories to another group or the whole class.

Group members will create an even stronger sense of unity when you task them with choosing a name for their group, developing a logo, creating a slogan, or otherwise establishing themselves as a core group.

STEP 3: Model engagement.

The third component of I-TEAM teaches students *how* to fully engage with the group to work toward learning and success. Engagement is not limited to participation. Communication is also necessary for active engagement; it extends to posing questions for clarification or exploring ideas. Here are a few ideas:

- Share videos of effective teams that have high levels of engagement.

- In whole-class activities, be mindful of how students are engaging and when some students are not. Your observations serve as the foundation to prompt students to be more engaged with their groups or to provide positive reinforcement for those interacting with the lesson.

- Model strategies like inviting others to speak to broaden how students think about engagement.

- Another overlooked action is students making an effort to understand what the group is learning. It could be paraphrasing, asking clarifying questions, or giving feedback to the speaker to repeat something or increase the volume of their voice.

- Recognize these actions and give credit for quality examples when they occur.

STEP 4: Role-play taking action.

Our goal is for students to contribute to the learning of others, and that requires some leadership skills. Group members should notice if someone is excluded, off-task, or devalued in any way. Inevitably, conflict will arise. It's expected and, as long as it's confronted in a way that is productive, is often beneficial in the end. A little resistance, disagreement, or doubt moves the dialogue into a direction of providing evidence, widening perspectives, and building confidence.

Children and adolescents are still developing skills to mediate and resolve conflict. Thus, we can anticipate the need for plenty of practice and reflection on how to maintain respect and dignity while facing conflict. Considering that many adults have never perfected this skill, we can expect that emotions might flare, tensions could get high, and problems will potentially grow. Rather than waiting for these moments and attempting to facilitate de-escalation while it is occurring, be proactive.

Provide scenarios when the vibe is calm and the conflict is disconnected from the group. Have students discuss hypothetical—but realistic—situations and provide multiple options for resolving them. Here are a few ideas:

- Some group members are on their phones when they're supposed to be working.

- Someone in the group is being bossy and not letting others share their ideas.

- The group is stuck and doesn't know what to do next.

- A team member says something rude to you about another student.

- There is disagreement about how to tackle the project.

STEP 5: Notice and narrate mindfulness.

Mindfulness means paying attention to what is happening in the moment without condemnation. Classrooms are busy places, making it easy to miss details that are worth noticing. On the occasions when you notice something and it causes you to reach out to a student, narrate what you noticed. For example, "You seem to have something to add, but you waited for him to finish his thought. That's respectful," or, "It's a good thing you asked that clarifying question because it prevented a big problem."

Be on the lookout for nonverbal cues like body language, facial expressions, and tone of voice that communicate how a person is feeling in the moment. When appropriate, identify those as well. It might sound like, "You're shaking your head. Do you have a different thought?" or "When you leaned closer to Brock, he began to share his idea."

OVERCOMING PUSHBACK

There are bound to be some hiccups along the way as you're strengthening teams and building a culture of collaboration in your classroom. Here are some misgivings teachers might have when they add an "I" to TEAM, and answers that may help.

Some students are natural leaders, so I always let them lead. Even leaders need to back off and allow their teams to experience success. Nobody likes a micromanager. Students who are drawn to take charge likely benefit from using their confidence to encourage others. Prompt them to engage or initiate delegation so everyone makes worthy contributions to the group's goal.

Students ask the teacher too many questions about the task. Many times, group tasks are complex and have multiple steps. This makes it likely that some steps will be forgotten. Instead of having a student go outside their team and ask you these questions, provide written directions or empower one team member to share the task. On the occasions when there is genuine confusion, such as when a necessary resource was forgotten, create a **Huddle Up** by calling one student from each group to receive the resource or message from you and deliver it to their team.

They might do it wrong. You have probably seen the acronym where F.A.I.L. stands for First Attempt In Learning. It's ironic that concern for students going down a dead-end path or not achieving success the first time they tackle something is so often presented as a problem. If students do it wrong, it's an optimal time to engage them in reflection so they can analyze what went wrong and learn from their mistakes. Averting failure prevents students from learning in a way that is more likely to stick with them than immediate success.

Not everybody is at the same level. Everyone doesn't have to be at the same level to offer valuable contributions to the learning. When you intentionally create groups, be sure to consider these differences. Will these students flourish when they are around others who can model the learning? Is it better to put them together and offer some small-group instruction and additional support while other groups work more independently? There isn't a single correct answer. It depends on your students, the learning goals, and the group dynamics.

When students require more or different support than the other group members, mindfully set them up for success. You can do this by pre-teaching some concepts with specific students so they have the advantage of familiarity, providing them with key information the group needs to elevate their status on the team, or empowering them as advocates for themselves and their learning so they will actively seek to understand.

> **Averting failure prevents students from learning in a way that is more likely to stick with them than immediate success.**

They learn better if I tell them. This is debatable. You might have the perception that they learn better. Certainly, there's an argument that they will receive the information more quickly when the lesson is teacher-led. The truth is that listening skills are weak. The lack of keen listening skills is the inspiration for Hack 9: Amplify Listening Skills. We know students struggle to listen intently. The argument to design lessons where they must rely on listening doesn't carry much weight. We simply cannot ignore the clear research that has proven over and over that active learning, productive struggle, and deliberate practice have a high impact on student success.

Not all students know how to learn. Exactly! As educators, we must remember that being a learner doesn't come naturally for everyone. Many people have to work hard to develop the skills necessary to acquire new concepts and information.

They'll miss the big ideas. Getting lost in the details causes learners to lose sight of the big picture. Encourage summarizing questions to direct thinking to a broader perspective. In my book *Hacking Questions: 11 Answers That Create a Culture of Inquiry in Your Classroom*, I suggest you Play the Broken Record by turning your learning target into a question. For example, suppose a divergent conversation begins with a discussion about ice erosion then moves to glaciers, which leads to a talk about the sinking of the *Titanic* … and before you know it, they are engaged in a debate about who should get in the lifeboats when a ship is sinking. When a guiding question is repeated over and over such as, "What impact do weather and erosion have on the Earth?" it redirects your class to the purpose of the task. Students might have to return to it multiple times along their journey during the lesson.

If I don't help them, they won't do it. Students can be conditioned to rely heavily on their teachers. This is a learned habit that has been perpetuated by well-intended teachers who work hard for their students to be successful. If you have designed tasks so students have everything they need to be successful, trust your planning. Use a broken record response like, "I'm confident you and your team have everything you need to figure it out."

THE HACK IN ACTION

In 2022, I worked closely with one school's ELA department. I visited teachers' classrooms several times, observed lessons, and then, together with the teachers, reflected on the lessons and identified how they could continuously strive to improve. One day in February, the department chair, Bob Roberts, and I had a conversation about the lit circles he was introducing. His students were already familiar with the four roles they would use to engage in dialogue:

Summarizer provided a brief statement of the text that included key points, main highlights, and the opening statement.

Questioner/Discussion Director developed thought-provoking, text-dependent questions and facilitated the group's conversation.

Connector linked events from the text to personal, local, or newsworthy events. They also related events or problems to other people, places, times, or texts.

Illustrator brought images or visions inspired by the text alive through drawing, sketching, or digital media. The pictures provoke a variety of interpretations that others explored before the illustrator described what they presented.

While students technically fulfilled the functions of their roles, we were underwhelmed with the quality of their discussions, summaries, connections, and visuals. The students needed too many suggestions to get something down and, in the end, Mr. Roberts knew his students weren't digging deeply enough.

We brainstormed and came up with an idea to have them critique the quality of responses for each role. He had a handful of sample summaries, written connections, discussion questions, and hand-drawn illustrations ready to go. In the spring, a new group of students was ready for their first experience with lit circles. Mr. Roberts was kind enough to adjust his unit plan so I could see how students responded when they were introduced to the roles.

The goal was for students to critique the samples on how others implemented their roles based on the descriptions provided. The roles were printed on small slips of paper that the small groups could easily manipulate as they discussed the quality of each sample. They had to rank the examples and justify why they thought each one was the best, worst, or in between. There wasn't a clear sequence from poor to outstanding. I'm not even sure the teacher and I would have agreed on the rankings.

But that wasn't the point. Instead, all the samples were pretty average, with each having one aspect that stood out as an effective approach to their role. Groups were required to defend their sequence and describe what stood out during their critique, making a list of exceptional qualities related to each job.

Students debated these qualities, backing them up with details like, "When an answer could be found in the text, it was too simple and wouldn't lead to quality discussions." The result of the exercise was clearly defined success criteria that distinguish good from superior examples of how to fulfill their roles. This is the list the class generated for Questioner/Discussion Director:

- Stay on topic.

- Ask complex questions.

- Expand on your responses.

- Make sure everyone gets a chance to participate.

- Have your own thoughts.

It was glorious.

We celebrated after class, and I told him about a year ago that I'd be writing about that day in my next book.

Teams are made up of individuals who share the common goal of learning. When we Add an "I" to TEAM, we emphasize the importance of self-awareness and personal accountability to the team's success. Members of successful teams work together, are fully engaged, take action to protect the group's culture, and are mindful of how their contributions impact the team's synergy.

Add an "I" to TEAM Reflection Questions:

- Why is it a problem that ownership of responsibility is missing?

- How does I-TEAM support this Hack?

- What are the steps for full implementation of the Add an "I" to TEAM Hack?

- How do you connect to the Hack in Action?

- How might the Add an "I" to TEAM Hack impact student learning?

Add an "I" to TEAM Application Questions:

- How does the Add an "I" to TEAM Hack align with your current instructional practice?

- How can you apply the concepts within the Add an "I" to TEAM Hack immediately?

- What self-awareness or accountability skills do your students already have?

- How will you encourage individual accountability in group work?

- How might the Add an "I" to TEAM Hack benefit students with different needs?

- How will you monitor your students' contributions to their groups?

HACK 6

KEEP TIME
Manage the Clock Effectively

Time is what we want most, but what we use worst.
— WILLIAM PENN, WRITER AND RELIGIOUS THINKER

THE PROBLEM: TIME IS MISMANAGED

TIME IS A key component to learning. Managing time is a constant consideration for all teachers:

- How much time will we allocate for this mini-lesson?

- How long will it take students to engage in an activity?

- What on earth will we do if there is a fire drill today?

Not only is time important when planning lessons, but it is especially challenging when executing effective group work.

Some groups finish early, while others don't finish at all. If one group depends on another group to complete its task, students are then waiting on other students, which is an invitation for disengagement and a classroom management nightmare. It is difficult to estimate how long new learners will need to interact with content, process it, and get comfortable with it. Add in student conversations, transition times, and opportunities for delays, and the time needed becomes even cloudier.

At multiple points in a lesson, time can be lost. In my observations of thousands of classrooms, I've noticed the scenarios when the mismanagement of time led to a plethora of problems. The four categories where time is the most vulnerable are shown in Image 6.1. Basically, we lose time because of the materials, complications with the routine or activity itself, students' interactions with each other and the teacher, or the pacing of the task.

How Time Can Be Mismanaged			
Materials	Materials are disorganized.	Routine	Students are unsure of the expectations.
	Resources are not accessible.		Directions are unclear.
	Learners are unprepared when they come to a group.		Focus is on the product not the learning.
			Transitions are slow.
	Too many bodies are in a single part of the room.		There isn't clarity on where students should work.
	Tools or equipment are broken or missing.		
Interactions	Students have multiple questions before and during the activity.	Pacing	Students lag in getting started.
			One big task with multiple parts is given.
	Teacher stalls productivity.		The task is more challenging than expected.
	Social conversations prevent focus.		
	Collaboration skills are lacking.		Students work at different speeds.
	There are behavior interruptions.		

Image 6.1

When we examine what conditions cause time problems, we see that some are easier to address than others. Viktor Frankl, a Jewish-Austrian psychiatrist, famously said, "Control the controllables." When it comes to managing time, we can prepare for and avoid some stumbling blocks, but for others, we need a back-up plan when they're out of our control.

THE HACK: KEEP TIME

It's impossible to manage time without being mindful of it in the first place. One question I ask teachers when they share their lesson plans is how long they expect each aspect of the lesson to take. How long for students to enter the classroom and get started? How long to transition into the mini-lesson? How long for student questions? How long for students to gather in their groups? It's common for teachers to struggle with these questions regarding time. Yet, when a lesson runs long, they have no problem identifying what part of the lesson lasted longer than it should have, cutting short the time for students to actively engage.

If a teacher doesn't have a goal in mind for how long it should take students to reorganize into groups, then certainly students don't know how long it should take either. When teachers don't clearly express their expectations for how swiftly students should gather their materials and relocate their seats, transitions can lag. I've never heard a teacher say they wish they had more time for students to move from one task to another. Shortening transitions is always a low-hanging fruit that maximizes the time students have to work in their groups.

Drawing attention to time and including students in its management produce multiple positive outcomes, including:

- Informing students how many seconds it should take them to retrieve their notes or book boxes makes them aware of time.

- Working with a clock creates a sense of urgency that they often need in order to keep moving at a lively pace.

- Tackling larger tasks by breaking them into smaller ones not only helps students organize their processes but also gives them practice with their personal time management.

Aside from lengthy transitions, one of the biggest time challenges in group work is the variance in the amount of time different groups need to engage in their learning. Lack of planning for early finishers results in the need to offer tasks to fill time for groups that work more quickly than others. When this occurs, it causes a dilemma. Do we hurry other groups along, potentially reducing the quality of thinking and learning? Or do we find a way to buy time for the groups still working by giving the groups that are already done another task? Neither option is appealing.

To keep quicker students engaged in the learning and prevent them from causing behavior issues, teachers need tools they can whip out of their back pockets at a moment's notice. Here are a few solutions to avoid having too much downtime for the groups that finish first. Choose the options that best fit your circumstances and the needs of your students.

- **Rank Responses**. Ask students to prepare to share the responses they considered but didn't ultimately choose. Of these responses, how would they be ranked for quality? What were they missing or why didn't they make the final cut?

- *Plan more than needed.* When you plan group activities, identify how many examples, problems, or responses will provide you with enough evidence that they have met the learning target for today. Then increase that number so there are more than enough practices for students. For example, if students are sorting items based on their magnetism and classifying eight of them would be sufficient evidence that they understand the concept of magnetism, include twenty items for them to sort. Once the last group sorts eight objects, you can end the task. In this scenario, nearly everyone will feel like they didn't have to finish the task. If students are inclined to complete the task, remind them the goal is to learn, not to complete an activity. If they've learned, they're ready to move on to the next step.

- *Create questions.* I'm a fan of exposing students to opportunities to ask questions—even if they don't get answered. The act of inquiring or wondering is a creative skill that leads to innovative thinking. Allow students to get curious about what they're learning by posing questions. Here are a few stems you can offer to model this type of questioning:
  - ► We wonder …
  - ► What if …
  - ► How about …
  - ► Imagine that …

- **Hand out answers**. When groups are doing an activity that has correct answers, be ready with an answer key, model, or sample of accurate responses. As some groups finish, you can quietly give them the answers so they can check their work and make any revisions they need.

- `Pair Out`. As some groups finish, one option is to pair up each group member from one group with another group member in another group. Allow them to compare their group's responses. Not only does this give each student more exposure to various thinking, but it also separates individual group members from their teammates. To represent the team's thinking, they have to understand it, so this option adds a bit of accountability for group members to be responsible for articulating their group's work.

- *Summarize for absent students.* If you have students who were absent, early finishers can gather materials and summarize the process their group used. Then tomorrow, when the absent students return, a process is in place to catch them up on what their group accomplished while they were gone.

- *Extend or challenge.* For students who meet the goal with ease, ramp up the rigor by extending the difficulty or complexity of the skill or concept they're studying.

- *Other tasks.* Some teachers have a list of options that are always in place for students who are done early. Examples include: check your work, read a book, do homework from other classes, or study. In elementary classrooms, they might add: practice sight words, clean your desk, read with a buddy, or play educational computer games. To support group work and to make future activities more successful, invite students to write questions for tomorrow's `Fan and Pick` or write a sequence for `I Have-Who Has`.

- **Join a Team**. Members of a group that finished way before the rest of the class can be split up and dispersed among the remaining groups. They can serve as facilitators (to lead the group without just handing over the answers), a resource (available to support when the group requests assistance), a communication collector (observe how other groups are implementing communication skills and provide them with feedback), or, if the task is different, simply join the other team as an additional team member.

WHAT YOU CAN DO TOMORROW

So many variables can cause your timing to be off. These suggestions help maximize instruction time and give you the information you need to accurately estimate how long different tasks or protocols might take:

- **Practice the distribution of materials.** Since there is no benefit to taking additional time to pass out papers and get supplies for a project, develop a system for how to distribute materials to students. Then practice it with a stopwatch, encouraging students to beat the clock. You'll be surprised at how quickly a class of thirty can pass out papers. The fastest class I observed got it done in under eight seconds.

- **Organize tools so they are accessible.** Some equipment is dangerous or valuable and must be stored in a special way. However, there are many supplies and resources that students need to access regularly. Identify a place for items like paper, pencils, and extra computer chargers. If they're behind a cupboard door, label where they are. Be clear about when students can use them, how to treat them, and the way they should be returned. If you require a checkout system, be sure students understand the process ahead of time so they don't need to bother you just to ask for an eraser.

- **Time activities and transitions.** Start paying attention and calling attention to how long various tasks or activities take. Let students know that a warm-up is expected to take three minutes and if they go over, take a moment to discuss why they weren't able to finish in the allotted time. It's possible there simply wasn't enough allocated time. In that case, the next day might have 3.5 minutes on the timer. But if the reason for not finishing in three minutes was that students were socializing for two of those minutes, then adjust the length of friendly conversation, not the time provided for the warm-up.

- **Display directions or expectations visually.** Group work often has multiple steps. Instead of repeating them over and over, post them visually so students can refer to them as needed. It could be a link on your classroom website or a slide you project on your smartboard. The idea is to eliminate the potential for students to stall because they don't remember the next step. Even if it only takes you one minute to notice their hand in the air and walk over to them, it's one more minute they could have been learning with each other.

- **Quietly observe.** While students are interacting in their groups, the role of the teacher changes: you become an observer. Every time you interject, even with a simple "How's it going?" you halt their progress and reverse their energy back to what they had already done rather than continuing forward. You move from the "you do" phase of the Gradual Release of Responsibility model to the more restrictive "we do." If you don't need to engage, then don't (see Hack 8: Practice Invisibility).

- **Use a visual timer.** Sometimes our internal clocks are waaaay off! Using an actual timer as a reference helps students get a more accurate sense of time, permits them to keep track on their own, and helps you avoid rushing them along. I have found my favorite timers by searching "online sensory timer."

- **Set timed goals for completing tasks or activities.** If you already create a daily schedule, try adding minutes to each portion of the lesson. Doing so gives you practice in estimating how long various tasks take and gives students the overall picture for the day's lesson. When minutes are assigned to partner or group work, larger chunks of time can be scheduled in segments by students. For example, how long do they think they should spend on each part of the task in order to complete it before time is up? You'll be pleasantly surprised to see that they'll get better at predicting how long it will take them. Additionally, if students gave themselves one minute to set up and instead it takes them seven, they know early in the time period that they are running behind.

- **Determine minimum and maximum.** Review the problems or questions students are assigned in their groups. Determine the minimum number of practices or applications students should engage in on that day. Then allow yourself to be content if the entire page isn't complete. If five problems are enough, then it doesn't matter if three are left blank. Let your students know they have provided sufficient evidence of success and they're ready to move on to the next step in learning.

- **Prompt students to repeat directions to each other.** When directions are lengthy, task one person in the group to repeat the objective and the process they will use to achieve it. Then, if there is any confusion, that same person will seek clarity from you.

A BLUEPRINT FOR FULL IMPLEMENTATION

STEP 1: Determine how much time is available.

This might seem straightforward, but an hour block of time doesn't usually mean a full hour of teaching and learning. Make note of every aspect of the lesson that will consume time: introduction or welcome to class, getting students' attention, sharing instructions, mini-lessons, powering up devices, gathering materials, assigning groups and locations, moving from one spot in the room to another, leaving time for questions, cleaning up, closing or reflecting on the lesson, and sharing announcements or school-related information. Some steps might occur more than once, so remember to include minutes for every time you share directions or students retrieve materials.

STEP 2: Estimate time.

Look at each piece of your lesson from step one and estimate how long each step will likely take. Even if it isn't ideal, initially, it's best to go with what's possible and likely rather than what you hope or wish can be accomplished in less time. It's common for teachers to underestimate or even leave out steps that require time in the lesson. This inevitably leads to lessons that run out of time for a proper closure. For example, if it takes your students five minutes to travel from one part of the room to another, don't allocate the amount of time you wish it would take. We'll tighten these transitions later. Oftentimes, we are unsure how long the active engagement portion of the lesson will take. It's okay to estimate high or low, but if you don't estimate at all, then you won't improve with being able to predict how long is needed for a lesson to play out.

STEP 3: Control the controllables.

After a lesson, review each stage and determine where time spent could be reduced with a routine, better organization, or practice and a faster pace. Start with one area at a time. For example, tell students your goal is for them to get their supplies and find their group within thirty seconds. Display a visual timer so they can see how close they are to the goal. If they don't complete the action in the time permitted, send them back to try again. The extra time to practice being expeditious will more than pay itself back in the form of quality time on task moving forward. Continue to tighten how time is used until students have fully maximized their learning time and you have a realistic but minimal goal for completing specific parts of the lesson.

STEP 4: Designate the amount of group work time.

Ideally, students themselves manage the time within their groups. Before checking their clocks, though, they have to know how much time they have and then determine a pace that allows them to engage in deliberate practice and active learning. If the time you give is short and the task is simple, there's no need to break it into smaller tasks. However, if a group's objective requires multiple steps, break them down one by one to isolate time segments. When learners can see which parts of a task are swift and which parts are lengthy, they are better positioned to make these predictions on their own in the future.

STEP 5: Segment group tasks.

When a group's work time requires five different steps, for example, the first time students tackle a learning task might require a brief ping-pong process. This means students do part one in their groups, then they receive feedback on part one as a whole class, directions for part two, and then they are released to focus on part two. This process of student groups to whole group then back to student groups again continues through each phase of the activity.

Ultimately, you remove the whole-class interactions. When groups are ready to manage longer blocks of time, lump parts one and two together. Eventually, groups will gain the ability to keep their own time. If one group is ready to keep the flow for a longer period of time, provide that larger block of time for everyone. Then, the groups that are still developing their sense of time management can receive your support in their small group. There's no need to hold back teams of students who need less of your time and attention.

STEP 6: Plan for faster-working groups.

Students work at different rates. Add in a layer of practicing soft skills, and that discrepancy can grow even bigger. Once groups begin to indicate they have met the learning goal for their task, teachers have a decision to make. Typically, it means rushing some groups while trying to keep other groups engaged. We can heed the valuable advice from Benjamin Franklin. He said, "If you fail to prepare, you are preparing to fail."

> **You can't add more time to your class period, but you can get more productivity out of the time you have.**

The lesson will run more smoothly and free you up to focus on groups that need support or to prepare for the next transition if you plan in advance what groups should do when they have successfully completed a task. Choose one of the options shared earlier in this chapter or otherwise decide in advance how you will handle faster-working groups.

A word of caution: remember that once a group achieves success, the extra tasks are not mandatory. Don't put yourself in a perpetual time challenge by feeling obligated to give early finishers time to complete an activity that goes beyond the lesson's original purpose or learning target.

OVERCOMING PUSHBACK

We can push back on time all we want, but it isn't stopping for us. Therefore, here are six thoughts, ideas, and perspectives on how to tackle time barriers.

It seems like the prize for students who finish early is more work. That perception is solidified when activities for partners or groups to tackle after the task is complete are presented as an afterthought. Instead, provide your students with a list of five things to accomplish, knowing that they really only need to complete three of them, with the other two intended to engage early finishers. It might take some getting used to for both you and your students to be comfortable with "incomplete" tasks, but when you focus on the journey of learning rather than on the final product, it's easier to forgo the need for additional work.

Everything is important; I want all students to do all the work. There are two angles to this pushback: the first is to assume that everything *is* important, and the second is to revisit what we deem *important*. If the task that groups are engaging in is necessary for them to complete in its entirety, then you are at square one with what to do when one group finishes early. This is where you offer additional related prompts or activities to maintain their engagement while the other students finish. Try not to present it as busywork. Nobody wants to do busywork, and your students will quickly question its value. Rather, offer them extensions or twists like "what if" scenarios to their learning. (Revisit this chapter's Hack section for more ideas about what to do when some groups need more time and other groups are already finished.)

Some events that throw off time are out of my control. That's right. Administrative interruptions, school events, intermittent announcements, spotty internet, and other unexpected activities can cut into your well-timed lesson. On those occasions, all we can do is roll with it and look for ways to minimize the impact these occurrences have on the balance of time. This is why we focus on controlling the controllables.

> **If we do not allow students to travel their learning journey at their own speeds, we risk robbing them of "aha" moments and the joy of overcoming challenges.**

It's not fair that some students have to do more work. If the extra work provided is irrelevant and clearly intended to give students something to do, then it might feel unfair. However, if the outcome is the gift of success through an added challenge and we embrace a growth mindset or strive to engage in productive struggle, then a fresh, learning-centered perspective prevails. Suddenly, your regret will be that not everyone gets time to move on to more opportunities.

My class periods are too short. The restriction of teaching within bells is a challenge for many secondary teachers who have multiple classes throughout the day. Unfortunately, this constraint isn't one that can be modified, so you need to accept the time limitation and plan accordingly.

One option is to segment the time students have to work in groups. At the end of one class period, they can gather in groups, develop a plan of action, and make a list of resources and roles each team member will have. Then the following day, when you greet them at the door, skip the typical routine of having them sit in their regular seats and send them directly to their groups. Explain the expectations and goals of the team's time, and problem-solve where needed. This will save you several minutes of repeating directions and transitioning into groups. You can't add more time to your class period, but you can get more productivity out of the time you have.

It doesn't matter to me how long it takes them. This is the attitude of a teacher who is focused on learning more than doing! We know that students learn at different paces and, if we do not allow students to travel their learning journey at their own speeds, we risk robbing them of "aha" moments and the joy of overcoming challenges.

Your first option is to consider how you might be creative with the time students already have with you. Adjust the task so students are intimately aligned to the learning target, or apply other solutions shared in this chapter. When you're committed to providing as much time as needed for students to interact with learning concepts and skills, you may be able to explore other ways to access time outside the allotted instructional period. Be careful, though: students aren't usually happy about coming back to the classroom during lunch to finish an assignment. If you're going to explore this option of adding time, do it with your students to discover their creative ideas for finding more time.

THE HACK IN ACTION

When working with the stellar fourth-grade team of teachers at Anderson Elementary in Trenton, Michigan, we developed a writing lesson to maximize time. Students were learning how to write an introduction to a piece of nonfiction writing. We call this protocol **Done and Run**.

The lesson called for students to work in groups of three. Each group had a paper with what looked like a pie chart, a paperclip, and a pencil. With these three items, students had a makeshift spinner (a digital randomizer would also work). The pie chart, shown in Image 6.2, had five types of introductions that the students had identified as ways to grab the reader's attention.

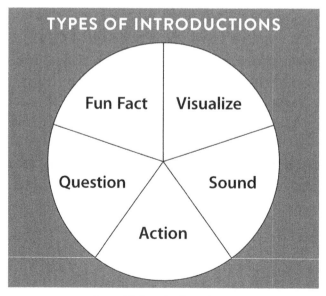

Image 6.2: Introduction spinner.

In the front of the room was a table with random topic cards. More than twenty topics, some of which are shared in Image 6.3, offered a variety of high-interest areas and subjects the students had previously studied in other content areas.

Tourism in Our State	How Internal Structures Help Humans Survive	Observable Patterns of Movement in the Sky
Summer Safety Tips	The Role of a U.S. President	What Minecraft Can Teach Kids
All About an Ocean Animal	The Rules of Baseball	Past and Current Threats to Tribal Government
The Use of the Five Senses	Cons of Owning a Pet	How to Make the Best TikTok

Image 6.3: Sample topic cards.

The teacher set a visual timer for twenty minutes. During that time, groups were to write as many introductions as they could. The spinner was used to identify the type of introduction students would write, and the topic cards provided the subject their leads were launching. Each introduction they wrote was considered a round. After each round, the students rotated roles so each learner had a different responsibility for each round. The teacher's goal was for each student to write three leads, so they had to complete a minimum of nine rounds during the allotted time. Here were the assigned roles:

Person 1: Spinner. The Spinner twirled the paperclip and announced what type of introduction the Author should craft. The spinner then validated that the finished introduction met the criteria for that type of introduction, including capitalization and punctuation.

Person 2: Runner. The runner went to the table in the front of the class and retrieved a topic card (returning the first card in round two). As the Author developed the introduction, the Runner wrote it down for the group.

Person 3: Author. The Author developed the type of introduction that the Spinner announced, using the topic the Runner retrieved. Authors created the introductions verbally while Runners transcribed. The Author made edits, and then the Spinner validated the work.

The roles were rotated, and a new round began.

Even though students were given ample time, the teacher watched the groups and ended the activity once every group wrote nine or more introductions. Some groups completed the minimum of nine, while others wrote seventeen intros. It didn't matter. Individually, students reviewed all the introductions their team crafted, chose the one they thought was the best, and explained to the teacher why it was strong. The group did not have to agree; this reflection was for each student to complete.

The beauty of this lesson was that students had repeated opportunities to practice the learning target of developing a strong introduction, they had examples they wrote and examples from peers, and they applied success criteria to determine which leads were the strongest and to explain why. I have no doubt that these fourth graders were ready to grab any reader's attention the next time they wrote an informational essay.

Lower Elementary and Secondary Adaptation: The same method can be used with older or younger students. Prepare multiple opportunities for students to deliberately practice the learning target. It could be solving multiple math problems, mapping different land features, or choosing various rhyming words. Having more than enough examples allows groups to work at their own pace without the pressure of who finishes first.

A key detail in preparing for students to work in groups is to determine how time will be allocated and managed. Precious instructional time can easily be lost in transitions, unclear directions, off-task conversations, missing materials, and unexpected interruptions. Even though some aspects of timing are out of your control, there are still many ways to keep time and manage the clock effectively. This includes minimizing the needless loss of time, maximizing group time, and expecting students to need different amounts of time to learn the same concepts.

Keep Time Reflection Questions:

- Why is it a problem to mismanage time?
- How does checking the clock and paying attention to time relate to this Hack?
- What are the steps for full implementation of the Keep Time Hack?
- How do you connect to the Hack in Action?
- How might the Keep Time Hack impact student learning?

Keep Time Application Questions:

- How does the Keep Time Hack align with your current instructional practice?

- How can you apply the concepts within the Keep Time Hack immediately?

- What time management skills or strategies do your students already have?

- How will you plan for groups that finish before other groups?

- How might the Keep Time Hack benefit students with different needs?

- How will you monitor the use of time during group work?

HACK 7

CREATE LIKE A CHEF
Taste Test Group Functions

*I tell a student that the most important class you can take
is technique. A great chef is first a great technician.*
— JACQUES PEPIN, FRENCH CHEF AND CULINARY EDUCATOR

THE PROBLEM: GROUP ROLES ARE ISOLATED OR IRRELEVANT

MOST PEOPLE ARE surprised to know that I enjoy reality TV shows. What is less shocking is that I love to cook. These two interests come alive when I watch cooking shows. In my mind, there is a progression of expertise in the kitchen. It begins with being able to follow a recipe. It requires you to have basic cooking skills: measuring properly and knowing the difference between sautéing and caramelizing onions, for example. The next step is when cooks can leave out, swap, or add ingredients to customize their entrées. This is where my skills lie.

But a true chef, like the ones I watch on TV, can create meals out of limited and sometimes odd ingredients. They have a sense of what flavors pair well together. Great chefs contemplate how ingredients should be prepped and prepared to produce a delicious meal. If I were given random and unfamiliar ingredients, I suspect the result would not be an exquisite dinner. I simply don't have the palate or the skills to concoct a tasty dish without a defined recipe.

Putting students into groups and expecting them to collaborate, think critically, solve problems, and learn is like asking them to make a dish out of Flamin' Hot Cheetos, eggs, chocolate chips, and ranch dressing. They've heard of all these ingredients but have no idea how to make them work together.

Using protocols to assign speakers and listeners or to determine who will verbalize the message and who will illustrate it offers students jobs to carry out. Engaging students in group work using these protocols makes their roles and responsibilities clear. In addition, these jobs are often highly structured, leaving little room for group members to stray from the expectations or not carry their weight. For this reason, tight routines (detailed recipes) are a little easier for students to digest.

Unfortunately, when not done well, this approach is ineffective for groups and often unpalatable. This is because when your lessons require students to collaborate, work together on a project, or engage in dialogue to deepen learning, there is a great deal of room for inequities in who is doing what and how they are held accountable. Open-ended and unstructured time for students to work in groups should be the end goal, not the starting point.

Assigning group roles is neither new nor innovative. My teachers used it when I was in school, and that was before the internet was available. Yet, simply assigning roles doesn't do much to lessen the problem of unproductive group time. Student roles within a group are unhelpful when:

Jobs are more related to housekeeping than learning. When students are in charge of materials or time, there is no connection to the actual learning. These are management tasks, and while they are important, they can be divided up among team members. It should not be someone's sole job to make sure the markers are put away or that everyone has a ruler.

There is uncertainty about how to execute the roles. Being granted the title of Word Wizard sounds fancy and organized, but if students don't know how to do the job, they will likely slide when it's time to perform it. I can easily imagine a student saying, "Does anybody have any words they don't understand? No? Okay. Next!"

There are no defined measurements of job quality. Fulfilling a role and performing it well are two different things. Without applicable examples of what makes one Questioner better than another, the impact of the student's job is not achieved at the highest level.

Responsibilities do not align with student strengths. Some students are gifted artists. Others have a way with words. People are often more engaged and motivated when they are able to use their strengths, talents, and interests in some way.

Completing a job doesn't lead to learning. When group work is parceled out, the parts do not equal the whole. If tasks are too isolated, group members might have access to a portion of the learning but not grasp the full picture.

The roles are not interdependent. Tasks that are interconnected require all the parts to fit together. Accountability is embedded, which brings a layer of expectations and pressure that are subtle yet obvious. If partner A didn't write the question that partner B is supposed to respond to, then neither of them can complete the task.

In the cooking world, these conditions equate to giving me a griddle to make soup: it doesn't do any good. There is more to creating a collaborative environment than assigning students to groups and giving them directions. The way they interact with each other requires the soft skills discussed in Hack 2: Talk the Walk. Even more important, the way students engage with the content requires cognitive skills such as thinking habits, strategy use, and content knowledge.

THE HACK: CREATE LIKE A CHEF

We want students to engage in group work the way a chef mixes ingredients for a five-star meal.

But before students are prepared to have full access to every ingredient in the pantry, they need to be familiar with each of them separately, much like how a chef tastes ingredients for quality and flavor. When is it best to use? How does it enhance other flavors? In what way is it prepared? What if you're out of a needed ingredient? How can it be served to others? These are the questions teachers take for granted when we design lessons for students to work independently. As experienced lesson planners, we recognize:

- when a specific strategy or skill can be used

- how a student's action enhances the learning of others

- in what way students should prepare for a group task

- what necessary skills or strategies students are missing

- how learning can be shared with others

We notice these needs because we have experience and understand the methods and steps that occur during the learning process. However, our students don't have that same level of expertise just yet. Their palates are not fully developed, so they need to sample methods to obtain, process, connect, and understand new learning. Once your students have prepared several recipes for learning, they can take some liberties with how they create their own learning.

Think of functions as ingredients for quality and productive group work. Students should taste test them so they become comfortable executing them freely. You can choose which ones you introduce to students and when. In addition, it's advantageous when your school offers a vertical alignment of group functions. If a fifth-grade teacher knows the students coming to their class in the fall have already learned specific functions, you can leverage the experience they already have and build on it to improve their palate for group work.

Instead of adopting group roles as if they're methodically following a recipe, your learners will become more like chefs, determining what skills are needed to spice up their learning.

Image 7.1 lists group functions that serve academic and cognitive purposes in learning. Use these functions to create your own roles.

Advocate	Critique	Evaluate	Predict
Analyze	Debate	Explain	Prioritize
Arbitrate	Defend	Explore	Question
Argue	Define	Facilitate	Represent
Articulate	Delineate	Identify	Retell
Assess	Demonstrate	Improve	Reveal
Build	Describe	Infer	Sequence
Calculate	Design	Inquire	Solve
Challenge	Determine	Integrate	Sort
Cite	Develop	Interpret	Suggest
Clarify	Discuss	Justify	Support
Classify	Distill	Locate	Summarize
Compare/Contrast	Document	Model	Synthesize
Connect	Draw	Observe	Test
Create	Estimate	Organize	Trace

Image 7.1: Group function list.

If these functions look familiar, that's no coincidence. These are the academic skills students are expected to learn and apply in content areas. When you combine functions to invent roles, it's as if you're creating your own recipes for interactive group work. Change up the functions so students can apply a variety of skills while learning in their groups. As these functions become more familiar, they will be staple ingredients the students know when and how to incorporate. Then, instead of adopting group roles as if they're methodically following a recipe, your learners will become more like chefs, determining what skills are needed to spice up their learning.

WHAT YOU CAN DO TOMORROW

Moving away from prescribed recipes or roles that leave a bad taste in students' mouths is not an overnight accomplishment. The following suggestions will get you started as soon as tomorrow so you can Create Like a Chef and provide fewer constraints within groups.

- **SING!** This might be the first Hack that has its own jingle: "Discussion Junction, what's your function? Hooking up thoughts, ideas, and concepts." Okay, that's my version of the *School House Rock* song about conjunctions, which some readers might remember. Whether or not you do, you can warm up those vocal cords and melodically remind students that discussions are about making connections from their own thoughts, ideas, and concepts to those of other people.

- **Clearly define your verbs.** A list of functions can be extensive, and possibly overwhelming. Familiarize your students with the verbs on your function list by using precise vocabulary within your lessons. For example, instead of using summarize and synthesize interchangeably, distinguish how they differ and how they are alike. When you synthesize, you summarize summaries.

- **Role-play good examples.** When students are learning the various functions, provide them with both high-quality and low-quality examples. These position students as observers rather than participants, and that makes them more comfortable with critiquing.

- **Divide up housekeeping tasks between everyone.** Students can do tasks to prevent wasted time (see Hack 6: Keep Time) and practice their soft skills (see Hack 2: Talk the Walk). If you need someone to be a timekeeper and someone else to be responsible for returning Chromebooks to the charging stations, include those responsibilities as add-ons to the learning roles in the group. It's okay to have students perform these duties; they just shouldn't be their only contribution to the group.

- **Label players.** Since we want students to apply cognitive roles in their groups, it's helpful to name the players. You can get fun and silly with the names or just be simple and direct. For example, in an Ask-Pair-Share activity, you might use A/B Partners, or you might use a compound word or a fun phrase like Rainbow (Rain + Bow) or Let's + Go!

- **Gather your ingredients.** There are skills and functions your students can already apply. Compile a list of the functions you can expect from everyone. This way, students are not limited to a single function that they can contribute to the group. Roles are made up of multiple functions. Increasing the expectations that everyone will make connections to previous learning makes their engagement more complex. Think about it—if one student comes across an unfamiliar word, do you really want them to sit and hope the Definer will point it out and offer a definition? No! We want everyone to serve multiple functions.

- **Emphasize how functions work together in games.** Take this tip from school leader Mary Kimball, Ed.S. She suggests linking multi-player video games like *Roblox*, *Minecraft*, and *Fortnite* and role-playing games like *Dungeons and Dragons* to how their groups will benefit from one another's strengths. Ask them to share how they choose between Luigi, who can jump higher than Mario, or Princess Peach, who can float. In the same way gamers value their characters' superpowers, group members learn to recognize and appreciate the individual contributions of their peers.

- **Assign functions to existing roles.** If you have already established roles in your classroom and students are familiar with them, don't throw them out. Elaborate on them by connecting the functions each role is responsible for carrying out. See a few examples in Image 7.2 that you're likely to be familiar with.

ROLE FUNCTIONS			
Leader	• Delegates tasks to group members. • Describes the functions of the other roles. • Integrates ideas from everyone. • Assesses group's success. • Prioritizes tasks.	**Recorder**	• Summarizes the group's thinking. • Documents the final response. • Manages time for the group. • Organizes notes and materials. • Traces progress the group makes.
Challenger	• Justifies responses. • Questions accuracy or reasonableness. • Critiques quality of the group's work. • Tests theories or ideas. • Reveals potential problems or conflict.	**Discussion Director**	• Facilitates group discussion. • Encourages the group. • Builds on ideas and encourages others to also. • Inquires about other perspectives. • Distills irrelevant information.

Image 7.2: Role functions.

A BLUEPRINT FOR FULL IMPLEMENTATION

STEP 1: Clearly define the functions.

Before you introduce students to the functions, be sure *you* recognize the nuanced differences between them. Do not use the name of one function to define another one. This would suggest they are synonyms, when each function is distinctly different from the others.

STEP 2: Comb curriculum materials.

The function list is not exclusive. Look through your curriculum materials for important verbs that would be useful functions for students to apply in their groups. Add them to the list, along with specific definitions.

STEP 3: Sequence the functions.

Determine which functions students already understand. Then select the ones that are relevant to your subject area and grade level. Collaborate with teachers from other grades to create a vertical alignment that determines which functions will be introduced, taught, or maintained throughout your students' learning careers.

STEP 4: Cluster similar functions.

When looking over the list of functions, you'll notice that some of them naturally go together. When students initially learn to execute the functions, provide them with responsibilities that are similar. For example, you could create a role called Einstein with functions that include: 1) predict strategies, 2) estimate solutions, 3) calculate accurate solutions, and 4) justify answers.

STEP 5: Create variety.

Once students get familiar with different roles and are comfortable executing similar clustered functions, widen the variety of functions a role serves. This will prepare them for when you later remove assigned functions so students have full access to any function their group needs, just like a chef has access to ingredients in a well-stocked kitchen.

STEP 6: Move to a menu.

Instead of assigning roles or functions, provide the list to groups as a menu for them to select the roles a task requires and to match them with the students who can perform those functions best or those who would benefit by practicing the skills. However, be careful that this step doesn't slip back into unequal contributions to group success.

OVERCOMING PUSHBACK

Teaching students how to behave and interact in a group setting is important but challenging. The following problems might cross your mind. If they do, here are some ways for you to resolve them.

Every student deserves access to complex tasks.

Some functions seem similar. They are. Many of them come straight from the standards we find in state expectations. When the standards include classify and sort, they intend for students to develop different skills. Similar … but different. Classify means to assign something to a category. Sort means to combine like things. Certainly, you might sort similar things and then classify them by category, but they are not the same function.

I already have roles established. Since functions are what students do in their roles, it's okay to keep the roles you already have. It will not take much effort to assign functions to the roles. Think of it as spicing up a dish by adding Cajun seasoning or adding texture with the addition of sliced almonds. If you come across a descriptor for an existing role that isn't on the function list, just add it to the list.

My students are all at different levels. That's one of the benefits of the Create Like a Chef Hack. When you cater to your students, you're customizing their interactions with the group. The important detail to keep in mind is that every student deserves access to complex tasks. Those who struggle tend to be relieved of challenging tasks in the name of helping them succeed. Unfortunately, this compassionate intention perpetuates the growing disparity in abilities. The students who need the most practice with high-level skills often end up getting the least.

Some students might not fulfill their functions well. Some of the skills are at a higher level. Instead of assigning simple responsibilities to the same students all the time, give the same complex job to two different students. When you're assigning functions to roles, you might have both the Leader and the Manager be responsible for comparing the group's product to the success criteria for the task. Think of it as a system of checks and balances. Now the group members have two perspectives to consider and collectively decide what parts of each example represent the group.

They don't stick to their roles. Congratulations! If students are freely using different skills to support each other and the groups are productive, then the roles are not needed. The end goal is for students to engage in a variety of thinking. We isolate the roles to allow students to focus on one at a time. If they are ready to expand the functions within their roles, you're successfully teaching teamwork.

THE HACK IN ACTION

In her classroom, Kellie Bahri, a fifth-grade teacher, administers a strengths survey to help students recognize their preferred learning methods and where they are likely to be at their best. Students take the survey individually and then interpret their individual results.

When Mrs. Bahri's students initially form groups, they establish norms, determine a team name, and engage in team-building activities like those shared in Hack 5: Add an "I" to TEAM. After they have had some fun together and comfort and trust are growing, students share their survey results with one another. Students enjoy learning about their classmates. Because the sharing is based on strengths, everyone is celebrated, and the results show where they can help the group succeed. And the strengths are not simply named: when students divulge that they learn best by noticing or following patterns, the group brainstorms tasks that would fit those group members' strengths the best.

I imagine comments like these in Mrs. Bahri's classroom:

- "If you notice and follow patterns, you would be good at organizing a final visual so it's easy for our audience to follow."

- "I wonder if you could use your ability to notice patterns to help us get out of a rut if we seem to keep doing the same things over and over again."

- "Would you rather have someone else take on the function of predicting, or can you use the patterns you see to easily think about what might happen next?"

- "Since you are good at noticing patterns, what else do you think you would be good at noticing?"

- "What are some areas you would like to strengthen? We can keep that in mind when we are delegating roles."

A helpful strengths survey for students, parents, and teachers can be found on the My Learning Strengths website. The simple results include a student's top two strengths and an area to work on … all emailed within minutes for free. In addition to giving teachers some insight, it's a great way to guide families' conversations about school and learning to focus on the skills that students have, as well as a fun way for family members to compare strengths.

Secondary Adaptation: This survey is also appropriate for secondary students. In small districts where students have been in school together for many years and know each other well, they might be able to predict the strengths of their classmates. Have each student create a slide that indicates their top two strengths. Then click through the slides and challenge the class to guess which student has those strengths. Students can add special skills or interests, such as being able to do a backflip or writing poetry to add some hints or help students get to know one another.

To be a great chef, you must be familiar with many ingredients and how they enhance each other. Group work is similar in that group members fulfill many functions that contribute to the group's overall product or success. Introducing students to different functions individually illustrates how each one improves the "flavor" of the learning. Students who are adept at a variety of roles can perform multiple functions that contribute to their personal learning and the learning of the group.

Create Like a Chef Reflection Questions:

- Why is it a problem that group roles are isolated or irrelevant?

- How do the group functions represent this Hack?

Create Like a Chef

- What are the steps for full implementation of the Create Like a Chef Hack?

- How do you connect to the Hack in Action?

- How might the Create Like a Chef Hack impact student learning?

Create Like a Chef Application Questions:

- How does the Create Like a Chef Hack align with your current instructional practice?

- How can you apply the strategies within the Create Like a Chef Hack immediately?

- What role functions do your students already apply?

- How will you embed functions into group work?

- How might the Create Like a Chef Hack benefit students with different needs?

- How will you monitor the quality of group functions your students use?

145

HACK 8

PRACTICE INVISIBILITY
Minimize Your Interruptions During Group Work

The greatest sign of success for a teacher ... is to be able to say, "The children are now working as if I did not exist."
— MARIA MONTESSORI, EDUCATION PIONEER

THE PROBLEM: INTERRUPTIONS PREVENT PRODUCTIVE GROUP WORK

TEACHERS ARE SOME of the most hard-working individuals on the planet. In fact, it's so typical for teachers to work as hard or harder than their students that they don't know what to do with themselves when group work is productive. As a school principal, I noticed that during collaborative learning time, teachers were continuously interacting with their students. Initially, I didn't think to question it. That's what teachers do—they teach, right?

I don't recall what triggered me to shift my focus from teacher instruction to student learning. As a school principal, I visited classrooms daily. Sometimes I stayed for a couple minutes; other days for an hour or more. I recall when our school first started working to improve our questioning strategies and become more student-centered. The goal was for students to do most of the cognitive work. What I noticed during collaborative learning was that teachers continued to interact with students, even if there wasn't an instructional or social reason for them to interrupt productive group work.

Image 8.1 shares the teachers' routines and structures, maybe habits, that I began to notice. Instead of making assumptions about how the teachers' actions were impacting student learning, we took a closer look. The results were surprising.

Teacher Action	Intent or Purpose	Impact or Outcome
Invite students to raise their hands if they're having trouble.	Provide students with a method for getting support when they need it.	Students raised their hands even when they could solve their own problems.
Approach working groups and ask, "How's it going?"	Gather some evidence of how students are learning.	Group progress halted. They paused their learning to recap what they had already done.
Roam the room, returning eye contact to students who look toward the teacher.	Offer non-verbal encouragement.	Teacher was drawn into group discussions.
Get the class's attention to give announcement such as "remember to …"	Share information to students quickly.	Group conversations are abruptly interrupted, and all students did not receive the teacher's message.
Stop groups to repeat and clarify a good question that one of the groups had.	Model quality questions, recognize critical thinking, inspire others to reflect.	Questions were not timely for all the groups, so the relevance was lost.

Image 8.1: Teacher actions during group work.

This unexpected discovery made me rethink my assumptions about teacher interactions. A lens of student learning shifted my focus from looking for quality teaching all day long and led me to revisit my beliefs about the role teachers should play during group work. Simply put, evidence of effective collaborative learning is students progressing and learning without the help of their teacher.

That's the whole point of group work—for students to learn from and with one another.

If students are trusted to be the drivers of their learning, with the teacher serving as an activator, a facilitator, and—on occasion—a guide, then teachers should be less present during student-centered learning. Of course, teachers are needed; they are critical components of student learning. That said, pulling back during certain activities delegates responsibility to students in a way that builds their confidence along with their learning.

THE HACK: PRACTICE INVISIBILITY

Even though people have a need to be needed, the most effective educators work toward being unneeded by students who are growing and learning. Since our students are still developing, the solution isn't for teachers to take a break and allow students to work independently without the presence of a professional educator. Instead, when teachers are virtually undetected by students, they have minimal impact on student-led activities while having full access to monitor, observe, and assess learning progress. Hence, they need to practice invisibility.

An invisible teacher maintains distance and chooses to interact with groups as a last resort. When you become an invisible teacher, you make the conscious decision to resist providing instruction and allow the learning you facilitated to stand on its own. During times when you're practicing invisibility, you restrain your natural responses to support, help, direct, or question.

The benefits of being less accessible to students are powerful. When you are leading instruction, these positive outcomes are more challenging to achieve than when you're practicing invisibility.

Benefits for Learners

- gain confidence

- build independence

- increase accountability

- learn from productive struggle

- grow comfortable with not knowing

- practice soft skills

- foster peer support

- encourage and develop leaders

Opportunities for Teachers

- gather assessment data through observation

- collect feedback on learning

- view the learning process

- note misconceptions and confusion

- limit scaffolding and spoon-feeding

- listen to conversations

- reveal natural thinking processes

> **When you become an invisible teacher, you make the conscious decision to resist providing instruction and allow the learning you facilitated to stand on its own.**

Your roles during times when students are collaborating and applying their soft skills to engage in active and interdependent learning are to observe, gather evidence, and assess. Here are five helpful tips.

TIP 1:

When you observe group work, it's helpful to carry a tool to document what you notice. It's challenging to remember everything that comes to your attention, and if you write it down or input it into a tablet, you're less tempted to share in the moment and break your invisibility.

TIP 2:

Before beginning, determine what evidence of skills or conceptual learning you will gather with anecdotes, checklists, or informal notes. Be sure to take advantage of your time to document abilities like:

- how students are progressing toward the learning target
- if they are applying the soft skills you communicated from Hack 2: Talk the Walk
- high-level thinking
- quality collaborations

TIP 3:

Consider writing down parts of the learning that are particularly surprising to you. If students find a task unexpectedly simple or challenging, it's worth jotting it down so you can reflect on it later.

TIP 4:

When your invisibility is high, you will have the opportunity to reflect in the moment and begin planning your next steps or adjust the closure you planned for the day. The more invisible you are, the more windows you have to consider differentiation, interventions, and other aspects of your instruction.

TIP 5:

Three conditions have the biggest impact on your invisibility: proximity, eye contact, and accessibility. Let's explore each one to see how your natural instincts as an educator conflict with shifting to a student-centered learning environment:

Proximity. The closer you are physically to students, the more likely that they will initiate interactions with you, even if they aren't really needed. As you roam the classroom when students are working together, don't approach their workspace. Stay on the outskirts and meander around as you collect examples to share with the whole class or observe students' application of learning.

If your classroom doesn't provide you with much room to keep your distance from groups, scan the room for hot spots. These prime locations are where you can stand and hear conversations of multiple groups at a time. When you linger there and are somewhat close to multiple groups, your presence in that neutral spot doesn't connect you with any single group. Therefore, the groups are less likely to assume you're close to their space because you want to engage with them.

Eye contact. There are significant differences in cultural norms when it comes to eye contact. In this case, we're referencing how eye contact is used as a means for students to nonverbally communicate that they have something to ask or say to you. When you return the glance, you agree to interact. In my observations, students simply looking at their teachers is enough to draw them in and break their invisibility. Eye contact is extremely impactful in that it can happen from across the room. At the same time, it's more controllable because you can avoid looking directly at students so they don't give you the "I need your help" face.

If you find yourself caught in a student's line of sight in an effort to get your attention, attempt to look away and use your peripheral vision to monitor their response. If it's more your style to exchange your own silent message, decline their non-verbal request to walk over to the group by shrugging your shoulders or shaking your head. It communicates that you're still invisible and they should review other resources before reaching out to you.

Accessibility. Refrain from establishing a norm that students raise their hands to get your attention and you'll come right over to help them. Your invisibility is compromised when you respond quickly to students' requests for your attention. So, take your time approaching groups. Even stop to tend to another task to further delay your interaction. If students solve their own problems before you get to them, there's no need to check in at all. Maintain your invisibility and do not interrupt them to hear how they resolved their issue. If it's important for you to know, write down a reminder in your notes to inquire about their success later.

It goes without saying that being invisible doesn't mean you completely ignore students and refuse to interact at all. Instead, I encourage you to provide the circumstances for students to use the resources they have (and one another) before accessing the quickest and easiest way to get information. When you're invisible, you can break your invisibility. But if you do, it should be a conscious decision to do so because students have exhausted other options or the social, emotional, or physical safety of students is in jeopardy.

Every time you speak, you interrupt student learning.

WHAT YOU CAN DO TOMORROW

There's no reason to wait to minimize interruptions for when students are working in groups. Here are strategies to help your students grow accustomed to depending less on you and more on themselves.

- **Turn when you talk.** The direction you face is where your eyes go. So, to avoid eye contact that lures you into student-to-student conversations, turn your body to face slightly away from students. Then either turn your head to speak or use the corner of your eye to connect. Then walk away. Another option is to look at the floor, the board, your notes, or anything except the students while they are talking. When they're done, give them a quick courtesy glance so they know you were listening, and start taking steps away from the group.

- **Give the thinking back to them.** Keep a couple of ownership questions or prompts handy when students ask you questions that they either know or have the means to know. Here are some examples:

    ▸ What do you think?

    ▸ If I weren't here, what would you try?

    ▸ You have everything you need to be successful.

    ▸ That's a good question. (Then be silent.)

    ▸ Where can you get an answer to that question?

    ▸ Who else might be able to help you with that?

- **Use visual directions.** Any time you give directions, but particularly when there are multiple steps with plenty of details, provide students a way to review the directions or expectations so they don't have to ask you to repeat them.

- **Encourage from afar.** Building relationships and encouraging students don't have to cease completely when you're invisible. Continue to provide positive affirmations or let students know you're noticing them from a distance. Offer a smile, nod, thumbs up, or raise the roof motion to connect with students nonverbally without breaking your invisibility by much.

- **Repeat announcements to each group.** Things get missed and plans change all the time in lessons. If you want to know if groups have completed a portion of the task, check in with each group rather than interrupt the entire class. When you check in, project a sense of urgency that you need to get to the next group so that you're not caught in a lengthy conversation with one group.

- **Save your words.** Every time you speak during group work, you interrupt student learning. The more students hear your voice, the more familiar it is. Save your voice for important topics like explicit instruction and whole-class lessons. Use other sounds like chimes, bells, or music to signal transitions. Point at your visual timer to indicate when time is running short. Reduce the number of fillers you narrate when students are working. Stopping a group's flow in thinking to hear the teacher say, "I'm seeing some good thinking," is counterproductive.

- **Math Work-Share**. This clever timesaver was described by April Parker, M.Ed., an elementary teacher and curriculum lead teacher. In it, she replaced the typical warm-up activity with one minute of a **Math Work-Share**, where math buddies reviewed their completed practice problems before turning them in.

  If there was disagreement or both mathematicians had doubts about the same problem, they talked it through together. When one student explained their strategy, the other listened with the purpose of following the thinking process and identifying any errors. Then they switched roles. Both students engaged in error analysis, looking for a silly mistake or a bigger misconception.

  Since implementing this practice, her class's math achievement has increased and the time needed for the teacher to answer questions has decreased. Basically, Mrs. Parker traded several minutes of teacher time for one or two minutes of student-to-student talk and peer support. Students with exceptionally good partner interactions got a ticket for class drawings of various prizes.

- **Start a parking lot.** To acclimate students to not having their questions answered immediately, start a **Parking Lot** that holds their questions. It can be a physical poster, part of your board, or a digital location for students to "park" their questions. Periodically review the questions to see if you find common themes where students are uncertain or if anything requires immediate attention, such as desired tools or confusion as a result of misunderstanding the directions. An added benefit of the parking lot is that you now have a record of the types of problems that students aren't solving on their own and are quick to hand over to you.

A BLUEPRINT FOR FULL IMPLEMENTATION

STEP 1: Clarify your role.

Students who are accustomed to their teachers interacting, checking in, and asking for updates while they are collaborating with peers expect you to serve in the same role. To avoid confusion, be upfront with what you will be doing—and not doing—while they are working. Clearly communicating that you have confidence in their ability to engage in the tasks with the resources they have (including each other) sets the stage for you being unneeded. If necessary, acknowledge that they might have to get a little uncomfortable if they run into snags, then repeat that they have everything they need to be successful.

Let them know that you will be observing and taking notes but will not be answering questions or asking about their progress. This is the ideal time to use Hack 2's Talk the Walk and let them know the specific soft skills you're looking to see and wanting them to practice.

STEP 2: Take note of proximity.

Take a look at where students are working. If they have choice seating, they might be spread all over the room, tucked away in corners, or—especially with young students—under desks. If this is the case, chart a path for how you will roam and where you can stand to maintain your invisibility but still listen in on students' conversations and look at their work without engaging.

At first, don't be surprised if students innocently break your invisibility. They're used to doing so, and it might take time for them to rely on their own knowledge, resources, and group members before reaching out to you.

The same thing happens on your side of the invisibility cloak. How educators interact in the classroom is ingrained in us. Most of our natural responses are not conscious, so as you practice invisibility, be mindful of how often you are tempted to approach working students and how they respond when you do.

Inevitably, there will be times when you don't realize your invisibility has been compromised until you're already in a conversation. Say, for example, that a student wants to share an "aha" they had. Try not to offer too much praise at that moment. Quickly allow them to finish their prideful share, make a note, then smile or nod and move away. While this might sound like you're expressing disinterest, you're not neglecting to affirm students altogether.

It's helpful for students to experience intrinsic satisfaction and receive accolades from their peers. When you are readily available with showers of praise, they won't seek it from their classmates. Additionally, learners who lack confidence look for affirmation instead of trusting themselves. Your invisibility provides the conditions for students to elevate one another and to build self-reassurance.

STEP 3: Be aware of eye contact.

Find a spot where you can cast your eyes. I tend to use my clipboard. I even doodle on it when I'm intensely listening to give the impression that I'm busy thinking about something else and not paying attention to the students. In the circumstances when you are pulled into a group or a student jumps in with a question before you can take two steps in the other direction, one trick is to just write down their question for later. At first, you might need to say something like, "That's a good question. I'll write that down for later." Eventually, you can maintain your invisibility by nodding, smiling, and making an exaggerated gesture as you write it down so there's no question you heard them. Most often, you're not needed to answer it anyway because students figure it out on their own.

If a student is eager to share their progress, write down their name and confirm that you are looking forward to hearing about it later. The act of writing it down breaks eye contact and turns your invisibility back on. While you're writing, begin distancing yourself so you're not available for another share or question that isn't necessary for their success.

STEP 4: Collect data.

Take advantage of the gift your invisibility provides you. Your observations of how students interact in groups or the strategies they apply when engrossed in learning are valuable. Hack 11: Go Live suggests what type of evidence to collect for assessment purposes while students are actively engaged in learning.

STEP 5: Choose to model or coach.

You will not be able to remain invisible 100 percent of the time. There will be times when you are legitimately needed to support student learning—even when the lesson is designed for them to succeed without you. In these scenarios, it's you, not students, who decide whether your invisibility should be broken. If you deem it necessary to interact, you can play one of two roles. Before you engage, decide whether you're going to model how effective groups solve problems or if you're going to coach learners facing roadblocks.

Option 1: Model effective group interactions. Even as groups build trust and confidence in themselves and their collective units, they will likely still seek comfortable options when faced with a problem. That "comfortable option" means you. If the issue that student partners or groups are having is one that you're confident they can solve through collaboration, then take the temporary—and I mean short, brief, fleeting, quick—role of one of their group members.

Focus on the interpersonal skills they're not maximizing and model them until the conversation has wheels again. If the problem seems to be that they have conflicting responses, rather than focusing on the content and the right answer, give them a jumpstart to wrestle with consensus-building or decision-making. That could be as simple as, "How might you come to an agreement?" or "What strategies do you have as a team to handle disagreement?"

When group members offer ideas that focus on problem-solving, you've done your job. It's time to activate your invisibility again and let them experience their own success. If you haven't experienced the power of shifting students from *what* they are learning to *how* they are learning, you have just hit a gold mine! The Hack in Action at the end of this chapter describes in more detail how modeling effective group interactions works.

Option 2: Coach learners. In most cases, this will be your first instinct. And at times, it's the right decision. However, to honor your invisibility and move toward being more intentional with your instructional choices, mindfully decide to break your invisibility because coaching is necessary. Otherwise, you'll slip back into being easy to access, when instead, you're trying to shift the ownership to students.

Coaching is when you provide support in the form of background knowledge, a brief reteaching, or cueing students to reference specific resources or tools that will help them. It could be defining an unfamiliar word that isn't part of the lesson, describing a setting that is unlike where they live, or directing them to a specific paragraph in the text that they should reread.

When I'm working with teachers, I encourage them to first recognize that they're coaching, then try a less-interactive approach before they jump into helping students. Instead of directing them to reread the text, which is pretty specific, prompt them to think about how they might get clarity by asking, "How can you be sure?" When you ask students to think about ways to justify their thinking, you're triggering them to think like a learner and to select a learner behavior. It encourages habits to swap between thinking about *what* they're learning and *how* they're learning.

Conversely, pointing kids to the paragraph in the text where they will find the needed information focuses their attention on what they're really learning: the next time they get stuck, they'll remember that the teacher is the best resource.

OVERCOMING PUSHBACK

I have encountered two reactions when suggesting that teachers practice invisibility. The first is relief and excitement. These teachers quickly see the benefits of being a fly on the wall in their classrooms. The other reaction is disbelief that it's okay, even beneficial, for teachers to reduce their interactions with students. Here are some of the initial reservations that may surface and responses to them.

I'm not doing my job if I'm not teaching. Teaching without learning is just educators talking. A broader perspective on a teacher's job is to ensure that students are learning. If they are, you're doing your job. This doesn't mean they're getting the right answers. It means they're grasping concepts and skills they can maintain and apply again and again. The idea that teachers should be working as hard or harder than their students needs to be squashed. Your heavy lifting occurs in the planning of lessons, not always in the execution of them.

My principal expects me to interact with students. Unfortunately, this is something I hear more often than I would like. Educators shift from teacher-centered to student-centered approaches at different stages of their careers. Since my experience as a student was mostly teacher-centered instruction and most people would conclude I turned out fine, there wasn't pressure for me to consider a different approach. Therefore, for all my years as a teacher and many of them as a principal, I had that same expectation.

If students were working in groups and teachers were silently observing them, I used to give feedback to encourage them to ask questions in order to activate higher thinking and rigor. Blah-blah-blah. The goal, in fact, is for students to ask *one another* questions to engage in deep learning. Try explaining these goals to principals and asking them to take note of how students are owning that role now. If they still contend that you should not be invisible, use research or this book to help them shift to student-centered learning and the power of invisibility.

To layer on the evidence for students to be doing the work of their own learning, look to your evaluation tool. Whether your school uses Danielson, 5D+, Marzano, or another structure, they all reference student ownership over teacher-led instruction at the distinguished or highly effective level.

Students will need my help. If you've designed a complex task, students *will* need help. However, it doesn't have to come from you. When you anticipate a struggle or confusion, ramp up the tools and resources the groups have access to so they can enjoy the victory of overcoming a challenge.

Sometimes I need to make an announcement. Change this to "Sometimes I need to tell every group something." The method for communicating to every student doesn't have to be an interruption in their learning.

Alternate options are:

1. Approach each group and wait for a lull in their conversation, then share your message.

2. Quietly share your message with one person in the group and ask them to share it with their team when it's appropriate.

3. Display the message in the room. For example, when they're finished, they should submit their work in Google Classroom and start their individual reflections. If students don't see the message and ask you what they should do when they're done, direct their eyes to the posted message without adding your verbal rehash of the written directions.

Observation data is not a grade. The first draft of this book's manuscript had nearly five hundred words in response to this pushback. I was able to reduce it down to one sentence: Observation data is more reliable, accurate, and valuable in student learning than grades ever will be. Period.

THE HACK IN ACTION

Students in a statistics class were tasked with interpreting data and representing it in a way that supported a claim. Then they were challenged to counter the claim using the same data. The teacher explained it to us as exposing how statistics can be skewed to favor a preexisting belief or confirm someone's point of view.

One student in a team of four, I'll call him Gregory, waved the teacher over. The teacher approached the group and listened to

Gregory's question: "Should we use the same type of graph for the claim and the rebuttal?"

The teacher was impressed with how his student was considering which ways of sharing information would be most powerful. Instinctively, he was tempted to walk Gregory through the pros and cons of dot plots, histograms, and box plots and then explore if scatterplots or regression would be beneficial. The teacher was interested in how Gregory would choose and knew exactly how to walk him down a cognitive path of thinking that would help him reach a decision. Instead, however, the teacher pulled up a chair and sat down. He paraphrased the question, "So, you are trying to decide whether the data should be presented in the same format or if it would be better to use different graphs." As he reiterated Gregory's original question, instead of looking at that student, which would close off the conversation, he looked around the table at the other three students.

Gregory confirmed that was their dilemma. The teacher paused, nodded, wrinkled his eyebrows, and uttered a quiet, "Hmmm," giving the impression that he was just as puzzled as they were, and he continued to look at the other students. He was modeling what he wanted Gregory to do: instead of asking the teacher the question, Gregory should pose the wondering to his peers.

It worked! Gina, one of the other students, took a breath. The teacher then gave his full attention to her. He even rotated his chair slightly to face Gina and away from Gregory. Gina began to explain her opinion. She felt using the same graph to represent conflicting data would be easier for the audience to interpret. However, she wasn't sure if they had the data to make it work. Another student, Ingrid, said, "I have an idea." At that point, the teacher glanced back at Gregory, then tilted his head toward Ingrid to signal he should listen to Ingrid's idea, then stood up and left the group.

Once the teacher had left the group, Gina, Gregory, and Ingrid made a plan. The teacher listened in from a few steps away and took note that the fourth student was not part of the decision-making. He made a note to set the Talk the Walk for tomorrow regarding methods of gaining a consensus that included everyone's voice, not just the majority.

Elementary Adaptation: This method can be used at any grade level. If a single student is serving as the voice for the group without actually checking with the group, a model might be in order. Consider how to model the collaborative skill they need: in this case, inviting others to share their thoughts. Step in for a few seconds to draw in other voices, then don't wait around for them to process their thinking. If your goal is to solicit everyone's ideas, then once other students begin to share, you've accomplished your goal and can return to being invisible.

Group work is largely intended for students to rely on one another to persevere through challenging tasks using collaboration. When well-intentioned teachers make themselves easily accessible to students, the learners naturally seek support and help, even if they aren't necessarily needed. Teachers who maintain invisibility activate learners and approach group work from the perspective that students have the tools and the knowledge to achieve success with little or no help from their teacher.

Practice Invisibility Reflection Questions:

- Why is it a problem that interruptions prevent productive group work?

- How does invisibility represent this Hack?

- What are the steps for full implementation of the Practice Invisibility Hack?

- How do you connect to the Hack in Action?

- How might the Practice Invisibility Hack impact student learning?

Practice Invisibility Application Questions:

- How does the Practice Invisibility Hack align with your current instructional practice?

- How can you apply the concepts within the Practice Invisibility Hack immediately?

- What predictions do you have about how students will respond to your invisibility?

- How will you maintain your invisibility when students are engaged in group work?

- How might the Practice Invisibility Hack benefit students with different needs?

- How will you monitor the impact of your invisibility on students' independence?

HACK 9

AMPLIFY LISTENING SKILLS
Apply Six Chinese Elements

*One of the most sincere forms of respect is
actually listening to what another has to say.*
— BRYANT H. MCGILL, AUTHOR, ACTIVIST,
AND SOCIAL ENTREPRENEUR

THE PROBLEM: DIALOGUE AND DISCUSSION ARE ALL ABOUT TALKING

CLASSROOMS CONTINUOUSLY PROMPT students to talk about the content. There are oodles of resources, even some in this book, that offer strategies to improve the way students communicate verbally. Sentence stems, vocabulary walls, graphic organizers, engagement protocols, and more all help students become better speakers. They improve clarity, sharpen articulation, and support language development. These are critical skills in sharing a message.

Yet, talking is only part of communication.

An equally important aspect of effective communication is listening. Nearly all the classrooms I visit address speaking, but rarely do I see a lesson that intentionally teaches students how to listen effectively. As I shared in my book *Hacking Questions*, being a good listener is different from being a good audience member. If

167

you have established expectations for listening in your classroom, pause for a moment and consider how active the learners actually are when they meet the criteria of a good listener.

Surprisingly, some commonly used expectations are not required for effective listening. Many anchor charts I've seen list checkpoints for students to apply when it's time to listen. They include details like sitting still, raising their hand to speak, and even keeping quiet. While these actions are easy to see, monitor, and request, they don't help students use listening to enrich conversations. It sounds more like how students should behave when the teacher is leading a lesson.

If we transfer these and similar definitions to group work, it becomes clear why the quality of conversations is low and students struggle to build and challenge one another's ideas. Just like we separated teaching protocols from content, there is a benefit to specifically teaching listening skills. Students need to know how and when to listen and then what to do with the information they gather through listening.

Students need to know how and when to listen and then what to do with the information they gather through listening.

THE HACK: AMPLIFY LISTENING SKILLS

Listening is not the same as hearing. Common dictionary definitions describe hearing as noticing sound or becoming aware of something through the ear. The distinct differences between listening as opposed to simply hearing include the qualifiers of gaining information or giving thoughtful attention. The Chinese character for listening, as shown in Image 9.1, illustrates the elements necessary to be a quality listener.

There are six distinct elements that, when combined, make up the symbol for the single word "listening" in Chinese: ears, eyes, maximum, one, heart, and king. Use these elements to teach students how to be active listeners so they can apply these skills when engaging in group work. Let's break down each of the six elements and look at their importance.

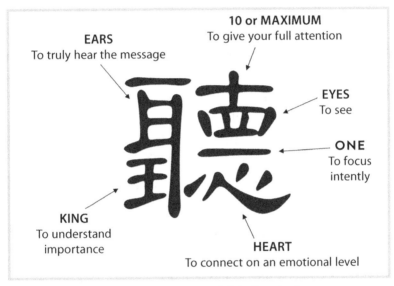

Image 9.1: The Chinese symbol for "listening."

Ears: Hearing the message is necessary when listening. When listening with their ears, learners should ask themselves:

- Am I able to hear the speaker's voice?

- How are my ears ignoring other noises?

- Do I suspend my own thoughts until I understand the speaker?

- Does the speaker know I understand their words?

Eyes: A speaker's message can include gestures, facial expressions, and visual aids. When listening with their eyes, students should ask themselves:

- Am I noticing what the speaker is communicating nonverbally?

- How are my eyes focused on the speaker?

- Do I understand the visual aids?

- Does the speaker know they have my attention?

Maximum: Above the symbol for eyes is the symbol for ten, maximum, or complete. It signifies that when listening, we give our full attention to the speaker. When listening with maximum effort, students should ask themselves:

- Am I focused completely on the person talking?

- How are my efforts designed to understand the speaker?

- Do I allow the speaker to complete their thoughts or ideas without interrupting prematurely?

- Does the speaker feel valued?

One: Quality listeners seek to understand what is being said. They think intentionally about the one message communicated. When listening with a focus on one, students should ask themselves:

- Am I trying to understand?

- How are my questions and comments clarifying my understanding?

- Do I already have my own opinion?

- Does the speaker feel I am hearing their one message?

Heart: Perspectives, opinions, logic, and emotions are embedded within a message. When listening with their hearts, students should ask themselves:

- Am I connecting with the speaker on an emotional level?
- How are the speaker's words accurately representing the message?
- Do I presume positive intent?
- Does the speaker feel my compassion?

King: In the presence of royalty, people show respect and treat them as an important person. When listening with "king" in mind, students should ask themselves:

- Am I suspending judgment?
- How are my words, expressions, and actions respectful?
- Do I have biases that impact my thoughts about the message?
- Does the speaker feel honored?

As you introduce these six elements for listening, explore how to adjust the way students are focusing, thinking, and responding based on their self-reflective questions. For example, when listening with their hearts, children and young adults might need explicit help and practice identifying positive intentions.

Engage in activities to reveal assumptions that people make about the reasoning behind a speaker's words. We all have experienced occasions when our words were misunderstood, triggering negativity from both the listener and the speaker. When listeners suspend judgment and give others the benefit of the doubt before interpreting their words as harmful or offensive, they consciously reduce the chances of conflict or miscommunication.

Calling out a key component of effective listening before beginning a conversation sets students up for success instead of reflecting after the fact.

WHAT YOU CAN DO TOMORROW

There's always room to amplify listening skills, so you might as well get started right away. You'll notice an immediate difference in how your students focus their full attention on the speaker and actively listen.

- **Develop paraphrasing.** One of the easiest ways for listeners to check their understanding of what they heard is by paraphrasing. A simple recap or summary of what the speakers said shows that their messages were received. This reveals any miscommunication or misunderstanding before the conversation gets too deep.

  Keep these three guidelines in mind when summarizing what a student heard:

  1. The paraphrase should be shorter than the original message.

2. Paraphrasing should be selective. Not everything has to be repeated.

3. The paraphrase should be in the listener's own words. It doesn't do much good to repeat verbatim what the speaker just said.

- **Prep students to amplify listening before a task.** During group work, Talk the Walk, as shared in Hack 2, by choosing one of the six Chinese elements and encouraging students to focus on it when engaging in discussion. Calling out a key component of effective listening before beginning a conversation sets students up for success instead of reflecting after the fact. If group members recognize that speakers didn't feel their messages were understood at the end of class, it's too late to tweak the interaction to focus on quality listening. It's better to amplify listening skills first so students can apply them in their teams.

- **Be specific when you prompt students to listen.** Offer a description of *what* or *how* you want students to listen. You can practice this during whole-group instruction, collaborative groups, or partner talk. Instead of asking students to simply listen to a text passage, ask them to listen for the emotion the author is trying to portray using their hearts. They can pay attention to the words, how they are read, and what is not said to get the full picture of the text.

- **Use the Triad protocol.** Several protocols are assigned to a listening role. The Triad is my favorite.

In groups of three, students are designated as a Responder, Questioner, and Summarizer. In the first round, you pose a prompt. The Responder provides their thinking, while the Questioner actively listens and uses questions to help the Responder add on or deepen their own ideas. The Summarizer doesn't speak until the Responder's time is up, and then they provide a recap of what the Responder shared. In the second and third rounds, the roles are rotated so each student has a chance to respond, question, and summarize.

- **Play listening games.** Sharpen their listening ears by introducing **What's That Noise?** You play sounds and have students identify them. Try things like boiling water, using a specific app alert, locking a deadbolt, and jingling keys. Another way to connect listening with thinking is to play **Walk & Stop**. Begin with students walking when the leader says "walk" and stopping when the leader says "stop." Then switch the commands. "Walk" means to stop and "stop" means to walk. Make it even more challenging by adding other commands. (Full descriptions and more listening activities are found in the appendix and in free downloadable resources at hackinggroupwork.com.)

- **Offer mindful moments that focus on listening.** Brain breaks and mindfulness are great strategies for helping students maximize their brain power. Mindful moments provide learners with practice in staying focused and avoiding distractions. This is most commonly done with various breathing techniques. You can get a twofer if you switch the focus to what students hear instead of what they notice with their breath. For example, play a song and invite students to isolate a specific instrument. It's usually easiest to start with percussion. Play the song for a minute or two and have students see how long they can listen to the drums without their ears being drawn to other instruments or lyrics.

- **Label speakers and listeners.** Perhaps the most common and easiest tweak is to assign A/B partners. Instead of launching elbow partners with "Turn and talk to your partner about ____," use your partner labels to direct student attention to listening. For example, notice how a small change shifts the focus to listening instead of talking when the teacher says, "Partner A, listen to partner B's thoughts about ____."

- **Distinguish active listeners from audience members.** There are circumstances when it's important to listen differently. If you maintain a single definition of how students listen, you might unintentionally be sending conflicting messages. Some teachers choose to label these different listening skills by separating how students listen in groups from how they listen during an assembly. Other teachers designate one skill as being a good listener and the other as a good audience member. However you distinguish each skill, students need to understand there are differences in how they behave when they are listening. The expectation doesn't always include being quiet.

A BLUEPRINT FOR FULL IMPLEMENTATION

STEP 1: Define listening.

Before you can expect students to apply active listening, they must first have a clear understanding of what it is and what it isn't. Review how listening has been referenced in your class before now. If there is the potential for confusion, such as when students should be quiet while someone else speaks versus when they should interact to communicate how they are understanding what's being said, then it's time to revisit these unique scenarios.

It's okay to admit that previous mentions of listening have been used in different ways. The point is to be clear on what skills are necessary for students to be effective listeners. For example, you might raise your hand to signal you have something to say in a staff meeting, but when was the last time you raised your hand to speak in an IEP? Raising your hand to speak is not always required or expected in order to be a good listener.

STEP 2: Introduce each element.

One at a time, visit each of the six elements found in the Chinese symbol for "listening." As you introduce how students use eyes, ears, maximum, one, heart, and king, call attention to how applying these elements helps them to receive an accurate message and engage in quality discussion or discourse. In addition, be sure to emphasize how a speaker feels when someone is truly listening. As students engage in group work, they will likely disagree or have conflict. In these moments, how they interact will determine the culture of your groups. Honoring their peers is a constant.

STEP 3: Co-construct success criteria for each element.

To help students understand the impact and importance of each element, develop details for examples of good and poor listening.

One way to ensure that students truly understand how to apply the six elements of listening is to describe what they would look like when implemented well.

When putting the six elements together, discuss with your students the mindset that effective listeners should have and how to apply these listening skills:

- **Listen intentionally:** What is the purpose of listening? Are they acquiring, critiquing, connecting, or applying information?

- **Explore personal points of view:** How do our life experiences, backgrounds, cultures, or attitudes impact how we receive messages and how we respond to speakers?

- **Choose responses:** How can we reduce our natural urges to interject whenever we feel inspired and instead carefully consider:

  - ▶ *What to respond to*: What requires clarification, sparks connection, or triggers inquiry?

  - ▶ *How to respond*: Will nonverbals help communicate confusion, interest, or curiosity? Is a tilted head, a lean-in, or a nod a better choice than verbalizing?

  - ▶ *When to respond*: Is the listener's understanding compromised? Does it warrant a clarifying question or request for more details? Will sharing a connection show disrespect to the speaker or enrich the conversation? When is interrupting acceptable? How does a listener know when it's okay to speak?

To reinforce the success criteria, you can role-play, have students self-assess, or have groups provide feedback to one another about how they are doing with their listening.

STEP 4: Select elements for students to focus on during group work.

Identify a listening skill and call it to your students' attention. Inspiration for what you choose can come from your observations during previous collaboration times, suggestions from students about what aspects of listening would benefit their groups, or simply a refresh to keep listening on students' minds. Assign areas of focus to the whole class, group by group, or individually. Within a single group, each member could be tasked with promoting a specific listening skill. That way, instead of only thinking about paraphrasing, group members remind each other to also focus on reading nonverbals and keeping an open mind to their peers' ideas.

STEP 5: Reflect on listening from two perspectives.

When students process or reflect on the effectiveness of their listening skills, encourage them to consider the benefits that amplifying listening skills has for both the listener and the speaker.

OVERCOMING PUSHBACK

Although learning standards everywhere include outcomes for quality listening, they can be challenging skills to teach. Here are a few barriers that might come up and how you can overcome them.

Some students have quiet voices and are hard to hear. If students are unable to hear their partners or team members, quality listening is nearly impossible. As students listen with their ears, if they are unable to hear the speaker, the rate of speech is too fast, or they don't understand details, the expectation would be for the listener to communicate that to the speaker. Do not allow students to use someone's quiet voice as a reason not to listen. Instead, it provides the perfect opportunity to let the speaker know what they are saying is of interest and that they may need to increase their volume to be heard.

If they're tracking the speaker, I know they're listening. Although eyes are a key indicator that the listener is hearing the message, it isn't a given. Some people can hear without making eye contact, and others might be mentally distracted even when they look directly at the person talking. This is why eyes are only one of the six elements of active listening. Continue to pay attention to students' eyes to see whether they are capturing nonverbals in addition to the spoken message, but be careful not to interpret eye contact as comprehension and understanding.

Group members don't stop to listen to others. Exactly! That is precisely why we can't just expect students to listen ... we have to teach our students listening skills and provide them with the opportunity to practice. Call attention to the benefits of listening, particularly when active listening helps someone understand a new perspective. This gives students a great example of how important listening is.

Assign learners one of the listening elements right before they engage in group work.

Another way to guarantee listening is to choose protocols that require summarizing, paraphrasing, or accountable talk like Agree-Build-Challenge [ABC].

Students often misunderstand the message when they paraphrase it. Miscommunication happens all the time. The purpose of the paraphrase in the first place is to pause and check that the message sent is received and interpreted the way it was intended. If there is a mismatch, the speaker and the listener should interact until they find understanding. Once in a while, students will share a paraphrase that's way off. In those circumstances, it's a great moment to highlight how pausing to repeat what is heard prevents the message from getting even more mixed up or completely misunderstood.

It's impossible to assess listening. Challenging? Yes. Impossible? No. If the purpose of listening is to understand what is heard while causing the speaker to feel valued, there are two angles to explore for assessment. The first is looking at how students respond when asked comprehension questions about what they heard. The second is focusing on the speaker. How did the listener's interactions in the conversation cause the speaker to feel about how the message was understood and received? Be careful that agreement or consensus isn't part of the measurement for effective listening. It's possible to understand a speaker's message and still disagree.

I want everyone to be heard. When lessons are engaging and students have high interest, everyone wants to say something about their learning. Many teachers want to give all students attention and respect by offering them time to share. You can provide the experience of feeling valued and contributing to a conversation through peer conversations. Certainly, students are eager to share their thoughts with the teacher. However, the more we normalize that sharing with peers is also a way to be heard, the more students appreciate speaking and listening to one another. When students are brainstorming or sharing personal experiences, it is an easy choice to have them serve as each other's audience.

THE HACK IN ACTION

In one pre-kindergarten classroom I visited, the teacher used action figures and plastic animals for students to practice roles as the speaker and the listener. It reminded me of when I was a little girl and would play Barbies all by myself. I served as the voice of both dolls as I created a dialogue for them.

The teacher in this classroom prompted students to do the same thing. They chose which figure would tell a story or explain a concept. Students used their own voices to speak for the action hero or toy zebra. Then, after the first figure spoke, they were to take on the voice of the other toy and paraphrase what was said. Pause and think about the brilliance of this exercise. Not only did students get practice with designating a speaker and a listener, but also through their play, students revisited the learning that had occurred in the classroom. The teacher had two opportunities to hear how students were interpreting the learning target, which provided her with double the chances to listen in on students.

By emphasizing the importance of listening through explicitly learning it, students develop the ability to hear messages using their ears and their hearts and minds.

Later, when we processed the lesson, I asked the teacher how else she used that play structure. She shared that as the lesson grew to support students to be active listeners, she would task students to have one of their figures ask clarifying or justification questions to the other. This prompted them to be more articulate with their semantics or to explain the evidence or reasoning for their responses. As students internalize these speaking and listening skills, they are prompted to transfer them with a partner and eventually in small groups and whole-class lessons.

Secondary Adaptation: Middle and high school teachers are not likely to bring out puppets or stuffed animals to have students practice their speaking and listening skills. However, the same idea was applied in a ninth-grade classroom when students prepared to interview community members. They planned questions and then predicted how an interviewee would respond. The reporter needed to use quality listening skills to frame a second related question.

Initially, the teacher's purpose was to help students develop follow-up questions. The goal was to start with a few questions but to let the interview guide the path for the conversation as well.

However, before students ventured off to conduct their interviews, they practiced asking follow-up questions in pairs. The practice in class gave students the confidence to move away from asking the predetermined questions that often felt disconnected. The results were interviews that had a natural flow because the student reporters amplified their listening skills to find interesting responses to explore.

In order for conversations within groups to be productive, there must be quality talk and active listening. The Chinese symbol for listening highlights six elements that we can use as a way to think about what good listening includes. Sharp listening skills build interdependence and a more collaborative approach to thinking and learning together. By emphasizing the importance of listening through explicitly learning it, students develop the ability to hear messages using their ears and their hearts and minds.

Amplify Listening Skills Reflection Questions:

- Why is it a problem to focus solely on talking?

- How does the Chinese symbol for listening represent this Hack?

- What are the steps for full implementation of the Amplify Listening Skills Hack?

- How do you connect to the Hack in Action?

- How might the Amplify Listening Skills Hack impact student learning?

Amplify Listening Application Questions:

- How does the Amplify Listening Skills Hack align with your current instructional practice?

- How can you apply the concepts within the Amplify Listening Skills Hack immediately?

- What listening skills have your students already mastered?

- How will you embed listening into group work?

- How might the Amplify Listening Skills Hack benefit students with different needs?

- How will you monitor the quality of listening skills your students have?

HACK 10

DEEPEN DIALOGUE WITH QUESTIONS
Deflate Conversation Crushers

Knowing the answers will help you in school.
Knowing how to question will help you in life.
— WARREN BERGER, AUTHOR OF *A MORE BEAUTIFUL QUESTION*

THE PROBLEM: GROUPS ENGAGE IN SURFACE-LEVEL CONVERSATIONS

S THERE SOMEONE in your life who seems to monopolize your conversations by sharing about themselves? Have you ever been in the middle of a story about an event at school, and these people interject to tell you about their own experience? We all agree that discussions that contain only declarative statements cannot build a connection between the two people talking as easily as conversations that include relevant and thoughtful questions. The same is true for interactions when talking about information and content.

Think back to a time when you asked students to explain to a partner how they reached an answer. When you really listen in on those conversations, you see that students usually just take turns telling each other how they solved a problem. The intent is for students to justify their answers and to hear how someone else went about their solution in another way. Yet in scripting hundreds of these types of student interactions, I have rarely heard comments about the partner's explanation. Perhaps more noteworthy is the lack of questions posed to the partners about their strategy or line of thinking. The result is an exchange that begins with partner A sharing, followed by partner B sharing, then both of them turning to the teacher and waiting for the next set of directions. Conversation done!

In student groups, your learners will face communication issues. I call them conversation crushers. Some of them deal with what students say and cause confusion, disagreement, failure to see relevancy, or opposing views. Other conversation crushers center more around what is not said. Some examples are limited thinking, not starting, getting stuck, or quiet students. When these circumstances arise, dialogue either spins or stalls. Review the following list of conversation crushers. If others come to mind, feel free to add them:

- **Information seems invalid or incorrect.** When statements are made in a group, they should be backed up with evidence or proof or come from a reliable source.

- **There is confusion.** Just because students have thoughts clear in their minds doesn't mean they have the language skills to articulate their thinking in a way that others can follow. When this happens, group members struggle to understand what's being said.

- **Relevancy is unclear.** Learning that has a purpose is much easier for students to grasp. If an idea or thought is shared, but others don't see how it connects to the group's purpose, there is a disconnect.

- **Thinking is closed-minded.** Once a possible solution or option is shared, students often cease thinking about alternate, perhaps better, options. In addition, some individuals commit strongly to their ideas and struggle to welcome other possibilities. Either way, dialogue shuts down before students explore all options.

- **Progress spins.** Fixating on a specific component, being overwhelmed with the complexity of the task, or just not knowing the best method for moving forward can cause groups to spin their wheels, preventing them from making progress.

- **Momentum stalls.** A focus on task completion leads to a quick agreement on anything offered by a group member that is "good enough." The conversation and thinking float at the surface level without going deeper because groups are in a hurry to finish.

- **A challenge arises.** Groups are bound to face struggles that require heavy cognitive work. Those who don't apply a growth mindset will struggle to overcome the challenges.

- **Group members are quiet.** It's easy to notice students who are vocal and to respond to their contributions. Students who are not as talkative can get excluded easily. It's quite possible that other group members assume the quiet students have little to offer just because they aren't speaking up.

- **Students hold differing views.** The backgrounds and life experiences of students come into play when learning is active. Students from a variety of cultures may have powerful perspectives to share. However, unconscious beliefs and attitudes can lead to assumptions. If these assumptions are not challenged, some viewpoints are not represented.

Overcoming these conversation crushers requires students to reflect on what is causing their struggles and to take action to tackle them. The best way to do this is through questioning.

THE HACK: DEEPEN DIALOGUE WITH QUESTIONS

Discourse is a key component of group success. Unfortunately, engaging in dialogue that stays on topic, particularly an unfamiliar topic, isn't as effortless as we might like it to be. Strategies that maintain discourse at a lively pace require students to justify, connect, and think flexibly. It's through quality questioning that dialogue is deepened and conversations are nourished.

We reap intrinsic motivation and drive when we tap into curiosity and inquiry.

If you ask students for the purpose of questions in school, they'll likely say something that relates to looking for right answers. In my experience, students share the perception that questions are what teachers ask and then students provide answers. This belief must change if students are going to interact in meaningful discussions. Questions, after all, offer multiple purposes in school. Notice that in Image 10.1, inquiry and metacognitive categories of questions turn on the most lightbulbs.

Question Category	Description	Examples
Assessment	Reveals what students have/have not yet learned. Aligns with learning target and success criteria.	• How would you explain _____? • What are the causes for _____? • How would you synthesize the information?
Engagement	Encourages participation or active learning.	• Who would like to share? • How will you think about _____? • What contributions will each person make?
Inquiry	Fosters curiosity and often more questions that lead to learning.	• Why do clouds come and go? • How does Amazon get my package to me? • How can I give back to my community?
Management	Addresses "housekeeping" type tasks.	• Is your group ready to begin? • Do you have everything you need? • How are you going to delegate in your groups?
Metacognitive	Prompts thinking about thinking.	• How did your actions impact the team? • How will you notice conversation crushers? • How will you maintain a sense of mindfulness?
Rhetorical	Does not expect a response. Often asked for effect or when an answer is known.	• May I ask a question? • Remember what we learned yesterday? • Will you remember to …?

Image 10.1: Question categories.

189

All the previous Hacks we've discussed in this book come into play when students use questions to push one another's thinking, gain new perspectives, and achieve a deep understanding of their learning. Ultimately, the learning they obtain will be used in similar but unfamiliar circumstances when they transfer what they gleaned in one setting and apply it in another relevant setting. These moments when the transfer of learning occurs are when we do the happy dance down the hallway and share the success. These moments bring pure joy to teachers. Nothing is more rewarding than cognitive lightbulbs clicking on!

A grand shift to increase the conditions that foster these moments includes a concerted effort to let go of the lead and hand it over to students. Lightbulb moments trigger pride, but at the same time, many of us fear giving up control. The worry is rooted in recognizing that teachers possess a highly specialized ability to ask powerful questions that students don't have the experience to pose. But … what if they could? Wouldn't it be a little less scary to turn over the reins if students knew when to ask questions, why questions contribute to learning, and how they could be asked?

The magic of questioning is revealed when the person asking the questions transitions their mindset from the expert to the learner. We reap intrinsic motivation and drive when we tap into curiosity and inquiry. These wonderings come from learners in the early stages of comprehending new things—not content experts who already know the answers. Their ability to actively listen (as shared in the previous chapter) is a must to build a group of inquirers. Otherwise, the conversation is crushed.

Question types and examples of how they could be worded to move a conversation along are aligned with the conversation crushers in Image 10.2. Being aware of the various purposes that questions serve helps us to broaden the types of questions we ask and to expand the impact they have.

Conversation Crusher	Question Type	Examples	Conversation Crusher	Question Type	Examples
Information seems invalid or incorrect	Justification	• How do you know? • How can you prove it? • Why do you think that? • What evidence is there? • What is this based on?	Progress is stalled	Launch	• What do we know so far? • What's the first step? • Where should we begin? • What are we trying to learn? • How will we approach this?
There is confusion	Clarification	• What do you mean when you say ___? • Can you explain that differently? • Do I correctly understand that ___? • Can you repeat that, please? • Could you provide an example to help illustrate? • Will you tell me more about ___?	Face a challenge	Strategic	• Where have we seen this before? • What strategies do we have? • How will our tools or resources help us? • How can we break this down? • What do we know/not know yet? • Why is this challenging for us?
Relevancy is unclear	Connection	• How does this relate to ___? • What's the connection between ___ and ___? • Why is this key or important? • How will this be helpful? • When/Where will this apply?	Group members are quiet	Invitation	• What are your thoughts? • Can you share your perspective? • Do you agree or disagree? • How would you respond? • Can we hear from ___?
Thinking is closed-minded	Flexible	• How can we think about this in another way? • What exceptions might exist? • Is this always true? • How would our thinking change if...? • How might this be viewed differently? • What's another angle?	There are differing views	Perspective	• What do we agree on? • Where do we disagree? • What's causing multiple viewpoints? • Are there multiple solutions? • How can we represent multiple views? • What experiences might be impacting our perspectives? • What assumptions are we making?

Image 10.2: Questions to overcome conversation crushers.

Inquiry and metacognitive questions are broken down into six types that combat the conversation crushers. While students don't need to carry around a cheat sheet to reference every time they pose a question to a classmate, studying questions and how they can be used in multiple ways enhances their questioning skills.

WHAT YOU CAN DO TOMORROW

Strategies for modeling questions and questioning for different purposes are widely explored in my book *Hacking Questions*. To make an immediate improvement in the quality of student-to-student talk, try these strategies that focus on the use of questions to deepen dialogue.

- **Let questions linger.** Sometimes I wonder if students think of their teachers as vending machines for answers: insert a question, and out pops an explanation or answer. In reality, questions that stimulate more questions and exploration are the ones that lead to rich dialogue. The next time students ask you a good question, even if you know the answer, let it float in the air for a while. Ponder connections and model inquiry by verbalizing wonderings about the question.

- **Perfect your think-alouds.** A think-aloud is when you narrate what your brain processes as you think. The intent is to invite students to listen in on how an expert thinks about a challenge. One thought inspires another as the person tries to make sense of a problem by using their knowledge and strategies.

It could flow in this way: "I noticed … and that makes me think … but I know … so, that must mean … therefore, my best thinking is …"

In her book *Think Big with Think Alouds*, Molly Ness reminds us that in addition to using "I" statements, think-alouds are brief, planned in advance, focus on something students are likely to struggle with, and cue the learners before it begins. During a think-aloud, the teacher is not soliciting students' ideas or responses. This is not the time for Q&A. Oftentimes, the think-aloud is a mental note to pay attention in the future to see if more clarity surfaces; it doesn't always lead to an answer. A think-aloud is a model that serves as an example of how students could think about a similar problem.

- **Take an inventory to search for conversation crushers.** Periodically pause when you're leading a lesson, walk through the conversation crushers, and verbally narrate if they are present or not. Your think-aloud might sound like, "I'm going to shift my attention for a second to make sure we aren't experiencing a need to justify our responses, make connections, or invite others to speak." The answer to these might be "no," but modeling how to take an inventory is a strategy you can ask students to use later instead of prompting them with specific questions.

- **Explore what an answer would reveal.** Edward de Bono, widely known as the originator of the concept of Lateral Thinking, once said, "Asking a question is the simplest way of focusing thinking ... asking the right question may be the most important part of thinking." To help students regard questions as inspiration for wonder instead of a quiz about what they already know, explore how an answer to a question would promote understanding. Would it provide evidence? Would it broaden thinking? Would it raise doubt? Exploring the outcomes of answers to questions emphasizes that questions have different purposes—even if their answers are not clear yet.

- **Critique questions.** When your students gather questions, either in brainstorming sessions, exit tickets, group collaboration, or other means, depersonalize them by not naming who wrote them. Then ask students to consider which questions are best. Note: you will need to define "best." One day, it might be the question that opens thinking the best. Another day, it could be the question that reveals assumptions. Perhaps they're looking for the question that offers the most interpretation. Giving students exposure to consider the quality of questions calls their attention to what makes a good question. The criteria they reveal can then be applied to the questions the students use to deepen dialogue.

- **Use student-created questions.** There's no need for you to do all the work. When engaged in conversations, students continuously pose questions. As such, they would benefit from polishing the way they craft questions. Encourage them to pose questions and then use them for discussions and in protocols that focus on questions like `Ask-Ask-Trade`, `Fan and Pick`, or `Back-to-Back`.

- **Label conversation crushers.** Share the conversation crushers in Image 10.2 with students. I bet they'll have their own conversation crushers to add to the list. Initially, students can use the table to help them get over the issues that are stalling their conversations. The benefit of introducing the conversation crusher labels with students is that it gives you a prompt to offer if they get stuck and don't realize it. A quick "Are you facing a conversation crusher?" shifts their attention from the conflict they're facing and directs it to how students are interacting. If the group members are facing a challenge or aren't seeing relevancy, they are triggered to identify the issue and have some possible actions to take to solve it.

- **Classify questions.** The simplest way to maintain a distinction between how students are learning and what they are learning is to divulge your intent explicitly: "Let's focus on *how* we learned today" elicits a different reflection than "Let's focus on *what* we learned today."

- **Ask like a journalist.** When you are leading class discussions, model how to pair listening skills with follow-up questions. Then state the obvious: "When you said … it made me wonder … so I'm going to ask a follow-up question, which is …" The narration of how you landed on the question walks them through the cognitive process of listening closely, thinking about what was said, and then going deeper. Just like journalists don't know the answers to the questions they ask, students asking explorative questions can take a conversation in a powerful direction.

A BLUEPRINT FOR FULL IMPLEMENTATION

STEP 1: Sequence the question types based on age and need.

Determine the types of questions that will benefit your students most. For younger elementary students who are eager to share their life experiences, you might begin with justification questions. They help your learners ground their responses in evidence and reliable sources. For older students, if you notice they are stubborn with their thinking and do not automatically explore multiple options, it would make sense to focus on flexible questions. Considering both students' needs and the types of thinking required within your units will help you select where to begin.

STEP 2: Describe conversation crushers.

Before actually using questions, students need to be able to recognize when they're needed. Focus on how a problem might surface when working with their partners or group. Have students developed a habit of seeking to hear all voices? If so, you should notice them using invitation questions. If voices are allowed to be silent, then students need to be more mindful of when their conversations are not making progress. They must detect the conversation crusher before they recognize the need to ask a question.

Just like journalists don't know the answers to the questions they ask, students asking explorative questions can take a conversation in a powerful direction.

STEP 3: Introduce questions to resolve.

Connect questions that are targeted to the specific conversation crusher. Image 10.2 gives examples, and your students may add to the list. The goal isn't to memorize the questions. Instead, by exploring types of questions, you arm your students with a variety of questions that have unique benefits to their discussions. Students, like teachers, tend to favor a specific type of question, so introducing entire categories of questions broadens their options to maintain quality discussions.

STEP 4: Sequence with `If-Then-By-So`.

The process students need to apply can be followed with an `If-Then-By-So` sequence. If (insert conversation crusher), then (determine question category), by (select a question), so (describe the outcome sought). For example, "*If* we do not agree on an idea, *then* widen perspectives *by* asking questions like 'What assumptions are being made?' *so* given facts can be separated from inferences."

STEP 5: Repeat steps 1–4.

As needed, return to different types of questions and use the same steps to walk through recognizing when they are helpful, choosing what types of questions combat conversation crushers, identifying specific examples of questions, and connecting the dots to follow through to the positive results.

OVERCOMING PUSHBACK

Flipping the questioner from teacher to student will require practice and undoing some students' preconceived notions about the purpose of questions. These are some potential arguments and how to address them:

Elementary children are too young to learn these question types. The purpose of exposing students to different types of questions is not for them to commit them to memory. The exposure and the added category labels provide language and opportunities for students to vary the way they view and pose questions when learning. If you like, create your own names for the categories and limit the questions to single examples. For example, retitle justification questions as evidence questions. Then select a staple question like "Where did the author share this information?"

Even when they know the questions, they don't use them. Get curious about this. Explore why students don't use questions when they are aware of them. If it's because they don't recognize when they're needed, then focus on the "M" for mindfulness in I-TEAM discussed in Hack 5. If you conclude that your students feel awkward using a reference or "cheat sheet," engage them in writing their own questions. An anchor chart in the classroom or a slide in an extra-large font provides a tool that students can glance at quickly if needed as an intermittent transition to internalize the questions. That way, they will be more likely to remember the questions without needing to look at them.

The questions they ask don't align with the true problem. First, celebrate that they're experimenting with questions. Then revisit ways to align questions that are likely to be helpful when conversations are crushed. A fun matching activity teaches students which questions help their group overcome specific problems. If you choose to challenge students with the matching task, be sure *not* to use the questions exactly as they're written on the resources they have. If so, they will rely more on their memory than their reasoning. The purpose of matching is so students will think cognitively about the problem with dialogue and what directly resolves that specific dilemma.

Asking questions doesn't mean they have answers. Think of it this way: good questions lead to good answers. It's a place to begin. Questions initiate thinking, wonderment, and challenges. It's through these processes that we achieve understanding. If they don't have the answers ... what other options do students have other than to pose questions to each other and themselves? Without questions, they're just stuck.

I am not always close by to prompt a question. Great! You're being invisible, just like Hack 8 promotes. The more you prompt, the less students prompt. If they have to marinate in the struggle for an extra minute, they have the opportunity to practice patience, perseverance, and a growth mindset ... all soft skills that learners need.

They get so wrapped up in the activity that they don't pause to deepen conversations. When you notice that students are focused on right answers and task completion, you'll likely be tempted to drop some questions that redirect their thinking. Instead of leading them right to water, contemplate ways you can inquire if they're thirsty. In other words, resist the urge to prompt students who have a shallow point of view in their conversation by asking, "Are there other ways to think about this?" That's the question we want *them* to ask. Instead, ask them to consider if they are in the midst of a conversation crusher and how they can use questions to overcome it. If they still can't see it, encourage them to conduct an inventory (described in the What You Can Do Tomorrow section of this Hack).

They just don't want to talk to each other. Humans are naturally social creatures. If students don't want to talk to one another, it's important to identify the root cause. Ask them directly or make some professional predictions. Then tackle the root causes to make their experience of working with peers less risky and more fun. Revisit Hack 1: Calm the Amygdala if the barrier is fear. If you're looking to add some fun and lower the risk, Hack 4: Perform Dry Runs is where you can find the best tips.

THE HACK IN ACTION

A first-grade teacher was building her learners up to engage in a Socratic Seminar. When I visited, they were still developing questions and ways to push the thinking of their friends. Before we entered the classroom, the teacher shared with me that she had two students who consistently monopolized conversations. She had tried a variety of strategies, including taking turns, timers, and inviting all voices.

The most success she had was when she used bingo chips to help students monitor their interactions. Each student received two chips. Each time they contributed to their group, they placed one of their chips on the floor in front of them. Once both chips were on the floor, they could pick one back up by inviting someone without any chips in front of them to speak.

As she explained her strategy, it sounded masterful! But, she confessed, it didn't play out the way she imagined. She spent more time reminding students to put their chip on the floor and pointing out when a friend hadn't used any of their chips that her class never achieved the flow she was seeking. I'm still convinced that, with practice, this strategy could be the perfect visual, tactile, and kinesthetic reminder that students need, but she chose another approach for our visit to her classroom.

In the lesson I observed, the same teacher tried something new. She chose the three most talkative students and assigned them to be monitors. Their job was to listen in on the conversations and put a dot next to someone's name when they shared with the group and a checkmark when they invited someone else to speak. The goal was the same: she wanted students to use invitations to ensure that everyone's ideas were heard.

The monitors were provided with a special pen and an official clipboard with a seating chart attached. The students engaged in conversation were seated, and the monitors stood outside the group to observe and gather data. It worked! After three minutes of group talk, a timer rang, and the monitors gave feedback on the evidence they collected for each member of the group. The feedback included non-judgmental data that shared how many times students spoke and how many times they invited others to speak.

One of the monitors was a young man the teacher was working with to be more mindful. As he reflected on the data he was sharing with his friends, he told his teacher that nobody ever invited him to talk. She asked him why he thought that was, and he said it was because he didn't wait for someone to ask him; he just said what was on his mind. I wanted to jump up and high-five the teacher right then and there in the middle of the lesson. But I saved it until we left the room and initiated a celebration in the hallway.

The teacher's clarity on the discussion skill of equalizing talk time and using invitation questions was strong. This sharp focus on the purpose helped her recognize that her initial strategy with the bingo chips wasn't producing the results she was seeking. Students needed to notice when their peers weren't heard and then offer an invitation for them to speak. When the first attempt didn't meet her expectations, she reflected on the challenge and created the monitor jobs.

Secondary Adaptation: This same idea can be used with older students. A Socratic Seminar uses inner and outer circles. Students sitting in the inner circle engage in conversations, and each student in the outer circle observes one of the students in the group. They then provide feedback, including praise for effective questioning strategies and suggestions on how to improve them. You can use inner and outer circles or embrace the monitor roles so students have an opportunity to step out of the group and observe how their peers engage with one another.

Conversations are shallow when they don't include rich dialogue and questions to deepen understanding. In addition, certain conversation crushers cause the group's discussion to halt, divert, or become unproductive. Using questions that align with situations that are likely to occur in discussion groups provides students with the skills to shift their conversations to be more productive and to deepen their learning.

Deepen Dialogue with Questions Reflection Questions:

- Why is it a problem that groups engage in surface-level conversations?

- How do the questions to deepen dialogue help address conversation crushers?

- What are the steps for full implementation of the Deepen Dialogue with Questions Hack?

- How do you connect to the Hack in Action?

- How might using questions to deepen dialogue impact student learning?

Deepen Dialogue with Questions Application Questions:

- How does the Deepen Dialogue with Questions Hack align with your current instructional practice?

- How can you apply the concepts within the Deepen Dialogue with Questions Hack immediately?

- What skills to deepen dialogue have your students already mastered?

- How will you embed questioning into group work?

- How might the Deepen Dialogue with Questions Hack benefit students with different needs?

- How will you monitor the quality of questions your students use to deepen dialogue?

HACK 11

GO LIVE

Assess in the Moment

Stand aside for a while and leave room for learning, observe carefully what children do, and then, if you have understood well, perhaps teaching will be different from before.
— LORIS MALAGUZZI, EARLY CHILDHOOD EDUCATOR

THE PROBLEM: ASSESSMENTS NEED CROSS-CHECKS

AS IF TEACHING students to collaborate, cooperate, and communicate weren't challenging enough, we still have to assess how well they are executing those skills. Assessment results serve as feedback to learners on how they are progressing toward a target, and the results come in various forms, such as grades, rubrics, written notes, and verbal comments. It's clear that assigning a B+ communicates something different than a one-on-one meeting about the strengths students have and the next steps for improvement. Even though there is an extreme difference in the effectiveness of these assessment methods, both the letter grade and the coaching conversation are considered types of feedback.

Several factors come into play when determining the best way for students to receive evaluations on their progress. Feedback on group interactions through traditional assessment methods like quizzes or written responses is rarely aligned to what you are assessing. A quiz might reveal if students understand the skills needed to engage in productive group work. Applying the skills, however, is a totally different story.

Here are five assessment questions to authentically gauge students' group interactions:

1. Who is performing the assessment?

2. What method are you using?

3. What are your criteria for success?

4. When are you conducting the assessment?

5. How will you use the results?

Now let's look at each of these factors a bit closer.

Who is performing the assessment? Evaluations of group work effectiveness range from group grades for a final product to peer reviews of their collaboration and self-assessments. While each offers valuable evidence, it's easy to see the problems inherent in them:

Problems when assessments are only provided by teachers

- Students don't own their progress.

- It's impossible to observe all individuals in all groups all the time.

- The criteria may not be clear.

- There are a high number of skills to observe and assess.

- Evidence of skills is often intangible.

- The feedback often comes after the group work is done.

- Content and interpersonal skills are two different variables to assess.

- Some group interactions are very short.

- Teachers must balance time between assessing, scaffolding, and facilitating group work.

Problems when group members assess

- Skills can be subtle and difficult to observe.

- Focus is on learning the content, not group interactions.

- Personalities come into play.

- Evidence of skills can go unnoticed.

- This invites blaming others for group problems.

- The Glows and Grows of the group include the individual assessing the group.

- Students undervalue their peers' assessments.

- If the end product is successful, students consider their group interactions as effective, even if they weren't.

Problems when students self-assess

- Student perceptions don't match what the teacher observes.

- They inflate their contributions.

- Learners don't know what they don't know.

- Single examples are not habits.

- Memory is cloudy and not always reliable.

- Individuals don't own conflicts.

- Evaluation of individuals excludes the unit's cohesion.

What method are you using? Exit tickets are not the best option for assessing interpersonal relations. Sometimes this confounds teachers because they believe that assessments must be concrete. So checklists, open-ended questions, reflections, and even peer scores are among the mismatched tools used to determine a grade for students' speaking and listening skills. Most teachers recognize these assessment methods are not ideal but agree that they're better than no reviews.

What are your criteria for success? There is no answer key for determining the quality of how well students build on each other's ideas. Without clear and defined goals for success, meeting the standard becomes a yes-or-no checkbox of completion, produces a subjective measurement, or—in most cases—isn't assessed at all.

When are you conducting the assessment? Limiting assessment, reflection, or feedback until after students interact also limits what students can immediately do with it. With a traditional lens of conducting an assessment after a student has performed a task or completed an assignment, the feedback for growth is corrective and comes too late to be helpful. The message is, "Here's what you did, and here's how it stacks up to what you should do." Of course, the evaluation could also be glowing, affirming, and constructive. Regardless, when you share the reflection and students perceive that the task is done, there is little they can do immediately to apply the input. At best, we hope that students will remember the goals they set and implement them the next time they work in a group.

How will you use the results? I would estimate that just under a jillion resources exist on this topic alone. My friend and co-author Starr Sackstein is a guru when it comes to the value of assessment to boost student success. Feedback, in any form, should help learners know where they are in the journey to meeting a learning target. Ideally, then, quality feedback leads to clear actions or goals the students take to continue their growth. If students interpret their scores, grades, or reviews to be the end of the journey, they probably won't use that feedback in an effort to improve.

THE HACK: GO LIVE

So, how *do* we grade group work? It's one of the questions that inspired this book because there isn't an easy solution. Authentic assessment is hard enough on more concrete skills and concepts like "Analyze how the authors distinguish their position from that of others" or "Explain why addition strategies work using place value and the properties of operations."

There's only one way to assess independent understanding, and it's not with a group grade.

When students are learning content in groups, we have the added responsibility of assessing their speaking and listening skills while developing their soft skills. On the walls of any Professional Learning Community (PLC) room, you're likely to find education researcher and PLC founder Rick DuFour's four questions:

- What do we want all students to know and be able to do?

- How will we know if they learned it?

- How will we respond when some students do not learn?

- How will we extend the learning for students who are already proficient?

It's the second question that stymies many of us. To tackle this conundrum of how to assess collaboration and interpersonal skills, we return to the five assessment questions to explore the options:

1. Who is performing the assessment?

2. What method are you using?

3. What are your criteria for success?

4. When are you conducting the assessment?

5. How will you use the results?

1. Who is performing the assessment? A cross-check between the students, their peers, and the teacher provides a well-rounded picture of how students measure up with the skills needed to engage in group work. When students complete self-assessments, they learn to recognize strengths, identify areas for growth, and set goals for improvement (see Image 11.1 for an example). Peer perspectives correlate with how students see themselves and how they're perceived by others. The teacher's assessment brings expertise in the area being assessed and their skilled observations. Each source of assessment—the students, their peers, and the teacher—brings a valued point of view that the others are not in the position to give. Therefore, a triangular approach builds in a checks-and-balances system with the goal of having them all align.

Listening Reflection		★★★★ ★★★★	★★ ★★	★
👂	I can be a good listening friend.			
👂🤚	My friend shares their story without me sharing about me.			✗
❓	I ask questions about my friend's story.	✗		
😊😊	I can share my friend's story with someone else.	✗		
😃	I give all my focus to my friend.		✗	
🕐	I wait until it's my turn to talk.			✗

Image 11.1: Self-assessment tool example.

2. What method are you using? When it comes to the content the group is learning, the assessments might be project-based. For example, if students are learning to create topical maps, then they should create a topical map. *However*, group work is designed to support every individual student's learning. Students work together successfully when they gain knowledge, apply skills, or understand concepts. The ultimate goal of their collaboration is for *each* student to meet the learning target, so students should be assessed individually.

Consider this example: Assessing a group's collective interpretation of a poem's meaning isn't helpful to anyone. Even individual summaries of how the group interpreted the poem are skewed. Standards and expectations for learning content are rarely linked to a specific application. To accurately assess whether students learned how to interpret poetry, they should interpret poems. The goal doesn't condition their interpretation of the poem to include prompting and support from peers. In most cases (some kindergarten exceptions exist), in order for students to be proficient or deemed to have met the target, they need to be able to execute the skill or show understanding of a concept on their own.

The skill students are developing in their groups isn't to summarize what they discussed in the group. Ideally, in group work, students practice soft skills and gain confidence. They deepen their learning about specific concepts so that they walk away from the group with an independent understanding. There's only one way to assess independent understanding, and it's not with a group grade.

Teachers whose content is mostly performance-based, like PE, art, and music, are accustomed to using observation as their primary assessment method. Since speaking and listening are skills that students perform, the assessment method should mirror the type of skill. It would be ludicrous for a band teacher to assess a percussionist's ability to maintain a steady beat with a paper-and-pencil exit ticket. It's just as nonsensical to measure how students engage effectively in collaborative discussions by asking them to write down an example of how they contributed to their group's discussion. The primary method for assessing the communication and collaboration skills within a group should be to observe them in action.

The question about collective grades or assessments is less rigid when the soft skill specifically involves working with others. It's clear that group assessments cannot completely replace individual feedback. Just because students were assigned to a group doesn't mean they all learned at the same level or contributed to the group's success in the same ways. Therefore, using group grades is inaccurate. Students might refer to it as unfair; as a data point, I would also label it as unhelpful.

However, there is a place for groups to receive comments that do not isolate individuals and give Glows and Grows about the group as a unit. For example, "When your group started to brainstorm, it opened thinking and led you to a fresh idea" focuses on the benefits the group enjoys when new ideas are valued and welcomed. Contrast this with more individualized feedback on the same group: "When Lanna's idea started a brainstorm session, it opened your thinking to allow for Troy's idea to surface as the one your group picked." The second feedback statement focuses more on the individuals than on the group dynamics.

Depersonalize your comments when you want individual members to see how the group was able to consider new perspectives because they embraced brainstorming without judgment. It doesn't matter who started the brainstorming, and it matters even less whose idea was chosen.

3. What are your criteria for success? With any learning target, students need to understand what success looks like. Just because a student asks a question to a peer doesn't mean it was a quality question or that it pushed the speaker's thinking. You only get the prize if your eye is on it.

You can share success criteria in many forms:

- A live or video demonstration of success

- A clear description of high-quality work

- A model for students to emulate

- A continuum of progressions such as rubrics

The success criteria should clearly state expectations for the depth of understanding or level of excellence. Knowing what the target looks like allows students to self-assess and reflect on their progress by comparing their current abilities to the success criteria provided. Image 11.2 is a tool to document evidence of observable listening skills. The first column describes the evidence you're looking for. The second column is for tallying each instance the skill was used. The final column records when an opportunity for the skill presented itself, but the student didn't apply it.

Listening Skills		
Evidence	Observed	Missed Opportunity
Engages the speaker with nonverbals.		
Shows agreement, disagreement, confusion, etc. in facial expressions.		
Interjects at appropriate times without interrupting the speaker.		
Comments connect to what the speaker says.		
Makes requests to the speaker when the message is not received.		
Asks questions to engage the speaker in more detail or depth.		
Paraphrases what the speaker said.		
Comments are on topic and do not turn the conversation to themselves.		
The speaker feels heard.		

Image 11.2: Single student listening skills data collection tool.

Additionally, Image 11.3 shows that you can reorganize the same information to focus on specific components of active listening.

Listening Skills Data Collection		
Student Name	Engages the speaker with nonverbals	Shows emotions in facial expressions
Aria	✓✓	
Anna	✓ ✓	✓
Bryce	✓	✓
Donavon	✓✓✓✓	✓✓
Elliott		
Nekka	✓✓✓✓	✓
Patrice		✓✓ ✓
Thomas	✓ ✓	
Zacharia	✓✓ ✓ ✓	

Image 11.3: Listening skills data collection tool.

4. When are you conducting the assessment? If it's an observable skill, assess in the moment. The ideal time to gather this information is when you turn on your invisibility (see Hack 8: Practice Invisibility). Another benefit is that when you take notes, it reminds students you are working on an important task, so gathering evidence reduces the urge students feel to access you when it's not necessary.

As your students develop their interpersonal skills, include a way to monitor the frequency they apply these skills. In Image 11.2, a column is devoted to noting when there is a missed opportunity. Compare the tallies of the two last columns to determine if the skill is applied consistently or inconsistently. Similarly, Image 11.2 leaves room for multiple sets of checkmarks: switching the color of ink adds another data point by tracking the observations over multiple days.

When you Go Live with your assessments, you are using what you see and hear as evidence of learning ... You have in-the-moment evidence based on actual student engagement.

5. How will you use the results? All this data is wasted time and energy if it's not used to make instructional decisions or to help students set goals. With data coming from three sources and across multiple days that align to defined success criteria, you have countless options for making good use of it.

Your options include:

- Compare self and peer feedback for alignment.

- Chart growth over time using teacher- and self-assessments that match.

- Invite students to interpret their data, provide examples, and reflect on previously set goals.

- Use students who need more focus on a specific skill as data monitors. Task them to gather evidence of students using the skill you want them to improve. For example, they might note how many times their team is paraphrasing, equalizing talk time, or not interrupting their peers. An example of this was shared in the Hack in Action section of Hack 10: Deepen Dialogue with Questions.

- Ask students to anonymously submit an area of growth and invite other students to brainstorm how they can improve that skill.

- Assign students to record a conversation on a tool like Flipgrid about what they learned in class. Then have them watch the video to look for specific speaking and listening skills they used successfully and those they need to improve.

Nearly every lesson offers an opportunity to gather data on student learning and group productivity. When you Go Live with your assessments, you are using what you see and hear as evidence of learning based on your professional training. This makes your observations valuable data that contributes to the overall picture of what students know and are able to do. You have in-the-moment evidence based on actual student engagement. And, as an added bonus, assessing with the Go Live Hack saves you from doing it later.

WHAT YOU CAN DO TOMORROW

Developing a comprehensive assessment system takes time. Still, you can implement tactics right now that improve your assessment data and provide students with quality feedback on what and how they are learning.

- **Provide verbal feedback on the skills you observe.** Give students Glows and Grows for how they are working in their groups. Take note of the language you use; it might come in handy if you need to create your own assessments or data collection tools.

- **Collect anecdotal data when you're invisible.** As you roam during collaboration time, take narrative notes about what you notice. Use a digital device like a tablet and create separate documents for each student so you are ready to conference at any moment. Your priority when you Go Live is to focus on what you cannot gather in other ways, so start by looking at how students are executing their group functions (shared in Hack 7: Create Like a Chef). In your notes, be specific, document the evidence you saw, give specific examples of what students said or did, and leave the judgment and interpretation for later when you're not Going Live.

- **Add self-assessments.** Teach students to be reflective by asking them to determine how close they are to the learning target. Follow up by asking them what it would take for them to progress to the next level so their reflection extends to how they can improve.

- **Arrange your room for dialogue.** Classrooms that are optimized for student talk provide more opportunities for you to gather quick data, even if it's during an elbow conversation. You can Go Live at any point during the day. You don't have to wait for a twenty-minute group activity. Design your classroom layout so students can engage in at least two different partners and a small group quickly and without much effort. If you have tables, that makes this tip easy. You have elbow partners (the person next to them), face partners (the person in front of them), and table groups (everyone at the table). If students are at smaller tables or side by side, their choices are elbow partners and the person in front of or behind them.

- **Gather baseline data.** It's motivating and rewarding for students to see how they progress over time. Begin gathering evidence of how groups are working together and share it with students. This provides them the opportunity to follow their journeys.

- **Have students practice giving and receiving feedback.** Some students (and teachers) are uncomfortable giving and receiving feedback. It's easy to be overly complimentary or too critical; you need to find the sweet spot so feedback highlights genuine and specific strengths yet also offers constructive suggestions in a compassionate way. Then during this practice, structure opportunities for students to give feedback on the feedback they received. Was it helpful? Was it specific? Do they know how to execute it? Do they believe it will improve their work?

- **Add observation data to your gradebook.** You might as well start giving your professional observations the value they deserve. Students who demonstrate they have and can use a skill or concept have provided evidence of learning. If you agree that the purpose of grades, mastery levels, or rubrics is to communicate how students are progressing toward what they are supposed to learn, and if they learned it and you witnessed it, then their grade score or level should include what you, as an educational professional, observed.

- **Conduct individual assessments after group inter-actions.** To avoid confusion about what individual students learned, assess the content skills and concepts of each student. Avoid collective assessments unless you're assessing collective learning.

A BLUEPRINT FOR FULL IMPLEMENTATION

STEP 1: Identify content and interpersonal learning targets.

When you communicate the academic learning goals for the day, include what interpersonal or social goals are the focus. On days when the primary goal is to offer explicit instruction on a skill like paraphrasing, it's enough to just include a learning target for the speaking and listening skill.

STEP 2: Triangulate assessments.

Students, their peers, and you all bring a different perspective to how students are progressing. When building listening skills, for example, peers are the most accurate group to share comments on whether they felt heard by the student listening. They can elaborate on why they felt heard and communicate those details to the listeners. If your goal is to have students align their self-assessments with peer assessments, cross-check what they're collecting to make sure it aligns. If the student is working on inviting others to speak, then the peers should have an opportunity to comment if they were asked for their thoughts during the group discussion. The same is true for how you assess. In order to triangulate it, you need to observe and give feedback on the same things.

STEP 3: Determine the best methods for assessing student learning.

Set your default to observe skills that students perform, such as listening and asking follow-up questions. There might be exceptions, but if your default aligns to the method that provides the most organic view of how students are applying their knowledge and skills, then you're conditioned to assess authentically.

Now, before you Go Live and assess in the moment, you'll need a system for gathering and organizing your data. Options include:

- Checklists that align with success criteria

- Single-point rubrics that describe how the skills should be executed based on your students' grade level

- Class list with blank space for your narrative comments

- Three-box continuum that provides a space for the expected skills that are not consistently present, skills students possess that are either expected or beyond, and skills that are logical next steps

- Glows and Grows template to document feedback for students

STEP 4: Go Live with your assessment data.

Your next decision is how to select which students to observe. One school of thought is to go down your class list and observe one student at a time. This ensures nobody is missed and you don't spend too much time assessing one student. The potential pitfall with this process is that when the next name on your list is a student who isn't engaged in the skill you are focused on, you have to skip that name and move on, making you return later to that learner.

Another option is to go where the action is. When you see a group applying their collaborative skills, find their names and start taking notes on the effectiveness of their teamwork. One suggestion is to start with students who are present but have inconsistent attendance or students who tend to be less interactive within their groups. These are the students you are most likely to have limited data on at the end of the unit, so it's helpful to frontload your observations of them.

STEP 5: Use the data to drive instruction and set goals.

The information and details you compile are feedback to you on the lesson you planned. Review them to determine whether your direct instruction was solid, the salient points were clear, and students were prepared for their task. Then look at the level of challenge within the task: Did it hit the sweet spot of what education researcher Professor John Hattie refers to as "not too hard and not too boring"? What does the data reveal about where to go next?

STEP 6: Reassess after you make instructional changes.

If the analysis and reflection you conducted in step five caused you to make changes to the unit, offer interventions, or revisit a skill or concept altogether, reassess to compare the before-and-after-changes results. There should be improvement, but you won't know if you don't reassess and look again.

If a different form of assessment is appropriate, like solving multistep math problems, include individual assessments so your data is clear on who has achieved success with the learning target. Remember, the goal of group work is to enhance individual learning and provide the conditions to learn and execute soft skills.

OVERCOMING PUSHBACK

Assessment and grading are two topics that are sure to ignite passionate conversations. Throw in homework, and now you have a party! Here is a selection of "yeah, buts" that are bound to pop up, along with my "yes, and" responses.

If I don't grade group work, students won't take it seriously. This is a deeper problem than it appears to be. Essentially, this pushback states that students don't care about learning; they only care about their grade. However, feedback is more powerful and actionable than a B-. In fact, the belief that students are motivated by grades only applies to a small percentage of students. Many students are actually discouraged by grades and don't put forth their best effort because they either fear their best isn't good enough or they perceive that good grades aren't something to brag about.

Caregivers want to see what students are learning. It's wonderful when school and home are in unison. If you have permission from the families of your students, grab your phone and take video clips of students engaging in collaborative learning tasks. Pop it on the school's social media site, or encourage students to watch it at home when they complete their self-assessment.

Students just score themselves high. This Go Live Hack lays out several checks and balances that would avoid this issue. If students score themselves higher than both you and their peers score them, then you have the makings of a great model for evidence-based claims. Think of it as how students can practice justifying their responses, providing evidence for their claims, and analyzing data to draw conclusions in a real-world setting.

It's not fair to give them a grade if they didn't actually turn in some work. Inhale ... exhale ... If students demonstrate they have met a learning target and their grades represent what they learned, then their grades should reflect that. How they demonstrate their learning does not have to be an assignment. A more open interpretation of "some work" should include interacting within their group and using the skills that cannot be translated to a tangible product for a grade.

Using all this time to Go Live on soft skills doesn't leave much time to grade the content learning. If you increase your invisibility and reduce the opportunities for students to pull you in to check that their answers are right, then you'll be able to find more time in the day. For example, you'll gain time from the less-important tasks like answering students' questions about what they're supposed to do, when they could be following the directions printed on the handout.

THE HACK IN ACTION

As a dual enrollment assistant professor who works with young adults, Brooke Oehme is keenly aware of how students come to her class with completely different views on learning and polar opposite preferences on how to interact. Over the years, Ms. Oehme has found some systems that work for her and her students.

She cross-checks student success by including systems that permit students to self-assess, receive feedback from their peers, and benefit from her expertise. As students plan for presentations, she positions helpful group interactions by sandwiching them around individual work time. When they launch a new project, her students begin in small groups with brainstorming. This gets their creative juices flowing. Students share ideas and are able to generate multiple possibilities in a short amount of time.

Brainstorming is low-stakes. There is no expectation that an idea will be used as it's provided, so suggestions are commonly explored, pondered, or discarded. Since only one idea will make it through to fruition, most ideas are not accepted. This causes students to not get too attached to their ideas.

With a head full of options, the next step is for students to contemplate their options, choose one, and get to work. The bulk of the heavy lifting and learning application is done individually in phase two. The sequence closes with students connecting again to reflect, to give feedback on one another's ideas, and to see how the project came to life.

On presentation day, three or four partners are assigned a group and use the DRE Method. D represents a Detail that stuck out to them in the final product, R prompts them to share their Response to that detail, and E is the Evaluation of how the response impacted their overall experience of the speech. As audience members for their partners' speeches, one peer provides feedback on the topic or idea, one on the presentation aids, and one on the citations.

Meanwhile, Ms. Oehme then handles feedback that is more personal in nature. For example, if a student is shy, that constructive feedback comes directly from her, using all the data collected when the groups Go Live. Observers take notes, and so does Ms. Oehme. She then compiles her notes and prepares a summary based on the data she collected as the student was presenting. Thus, students demonstrate their speech and presentation skills and are assessed on their abilities.

Elementary Adaptation: A brilliant management detail is that this teacher uses small groups to teach students to observe one another and collect data. In elementary school, this is a good option so students are not overwhelmed with twenty-four data points. From a best-practice perspective, groups of three or four are manageable to provide students with a small but captive audience that could easily engage in multiple rehearsals of their presentations in their groups before it's showtime. The assessment document can be grade-appropriate and give students concrete skills to notice and share data. For example, instead of DRE, lower elementary students observe if the speaker projected their voice and if their presentation includes a reference to the author's work. Those look-fors are easily swapped as your focus changes.

Too often, teachers rely on artifacts, usually produced by students, as evidence of learning. The word "assessment" triggers an assumption that learning has concluded and it's time to test. Rather than pausing or ending learning, teachers can get live data by observing students and using the information gathered during group discussions to provide evidence of learning and application of it. Since the end goal is for students to apply their learning, it makes sense to take note of when students are successfully using what they learned in real time.

Go Live Reflection Questions:

- Why is it a problem that students aren't involved in their own assessment?

- How does assessing in the moment help you to Go Live?

- What are the steps for full implementation of the Go Live Hack?

- How do you connect to the Hack in Action?

- How might going live impact student learning?

Go Live Application Questions:

- How does the Go Live Hack align with your current instructional practice?

- How can you apply the concepts within the Go Live Hack immediately?

- What experiences do students already have with self-assessments and peer assessments?

- How will you embed cross-checking assessments into group work?

- How might the Go Live Hack benefit students with different needs?

- How will you monitor the impact of cross-checking assessments when you Go Live?

CONCLUSION

Coming together is a beginning. Keeping together is progress. Working together is success.
— HENRY FORD, AMERICAN INDUSTRIALIST

STUDENT COLLABORATION MUST be purposeful and intentional. However, pausing for a moment of collaboration, accountability, or just a check-in requires premeditated thought and planning. There are plenty of challenges to group work that leave both you and your students frustrated, such as:

- If groups are too small, there are not enough shared ideas or perspectives.

- If groups are too large, not everyone has an opportunity to actively engage.

- When time is too short, thinking is incomplete.

- When there is too much time, group members get restless.

- If the task is too simple, collaboration is shallow.

- If the task is too complex, collaboration stalls.

- Students who like their peer partners get off-topic.

- Students who dislike their peer partners work in isolation.

All of these factors lead to many classrooms limiting the amount of time allocated for students to learn from one another. There is no question that teacher-centered, highly structured classrooms are easier to plan and manage. However, when it comes to student achievement, the goal isn't to design lessons that take a lockstep approach to learning. Employers are not looking to hire people who work in a bubble and follow directions well. There may be some jobs that require careful attention to procedure, but even in these environments, problems are bound to surface. And when they do, the rock stars are the employees who can problem-solve, collaborate with others, and effectively communicate.

Teacher-centered whole-group instruction, day after day, doesn't develop these vital skills.

So many components can make group work productive. If any one of these details goes amuck, the entire experience can flop. In the preceding chapters of *Hacking Group Work*, we unpacked the reasons group work doesn't always succeed and how to solve those problems. When students claim not to love reading, we look for ways to spark their interest. If they announce they detest math, teachers support a growth mindset so students will embrace their opportunities to learn.

Just so, if group work gets a bad rap, students might push back, request to work alone, or flat-out refuse to engage. Instead of limiting opportunities to develop and practice social and interpersonal skills, you now have the knowledge and tools to design lessons so that collaboration is relevant, helpful, and even fun.

APPENDIX

HERE YOU WILL find an alphabetical list of all sixty-five protocols mentioned in *Hacking Group Work*, along with their descriptions. Many include downloadables, which you can access for free on hackinggroupwork.com.

2-Minute Jar: Give students an image of a jar with gumballs. Share a prompt and invite students to color in one gumball for every example they can think of that fits the prompt. Suggestions:

- Different ways to greet someone
- Everything you know about ____
- Traits you like about yourself
- Things you are grateful for
- What you can do if you get stuck on a problem (Free downloadable image.)

3-2-1: Bring students' attention to what they're learning, how they're learning it, and where they will go next. 3 things I learned, 2 ways the group supported my learning, 1 question or 1 wish I have about the content or our group.

A/B Partners: Provide more structure to partner talks by assigning A and B partners. The added detail makes it possible for you to signal which student should speak first, who will share, what specific cognitive tasks are assigned to the student, and much more. With A/B partners, the engagement can be more equalized by alternating the functions or roles of each partner. Some teachers have more creative names like Peanut Butter and Jelly or Knick and Knack.

ABC (Agree-Build-Challenge): As you introduce student talk stems, start with three. A: I agree with your thinking. B: I want to build on what you said. C: I need to challenge your idea. Then as you add other ways to ABC, add them to the proper category. If a student says they respectfully disagree with a peer, that new sentence stem can be aligned with C: I need to challenge your idea. (Free downloadable poster.)

Affinity Mapping: To help students organize a list of thoughts or ideas, use this categorization structure. Each idea is written on a separate sticky note. It is important not to put more than one idea on each note. After the group has collected all their thoughts, they should sort the sticky notes and place those that are similar together. Do not provide students with names for the categories. Instead, they determine the most appropriate label for the groups they develop. This helps students identify bigger ideas from smaller ones. An example of this activity is detailed in the Hack in Action found in Hack 2.

Air Fives: To set a lively pace and engage in quick interactions, play upbeat music and ask students to roam around the room, giving air fives to their classmates. When the music stops, pause for a brief standing conversation. This process can be done once to provide a movement and check-in break or may be repeated to expose students to multiple points of view or to consider a variety of questions or prompts.

Around the Clock: Arrange students in an inner and an outer circle. The inner circle faces outward while the outer circle students face inward, creating temporary talking partners. Launch a question or prompt and provide sufficient time for pairs to discuss. Then, rotate the inner circle clockwise, symbolically moving ahead an hour. If you need to skip a contentious pairing, simply ask them to move two hours ahead, skipping the very next partner. With their new time partner, launch a new conversation.

Ask-Ask-Trade: Provide a question or fact for each student and pair them up with a partner. The first partner asks the second partner to respond to the question or provide information about the fact. Next, the second partner does the same. After both partners have discussed or asked their questions, they trade questions and find new partners. This strategy is versatile because it's great at activating prior knowledge, revisiting key ideas from a lesson, or simply engaging students in the lesson.

Ask-Pair-Share: Emphasize the power of questions with a protocol that stimulates students to focus on their curiosity and wonderings. Provide time for students to brainstorm questions they have about the content or about what has been shared by others. Then they pair up with a partner to pose the questions. It's likely they will jump to answering or interacting with each other's questions. That's fine; however, the purpose is to explore questions that impact thinking, so when it comes time to share, try to keep the main focus on how helpful questions are to deepen understanding. Share the most effective questions and let them linger without students feeling obligated to answer them.

Back-to-Back and Face-to-Face: Two students stand back-to-back so they cannot see each other. Pose a question to the entire class and provide sufficient think time for the partners to prepare to share their responses. During the think time, students remain with their backs facing their partners. When you give the signal (a direction or a sound), students turn around to face their partners and discuss the prompt. After a given time (45–90 seconds is often a good start), cue students to return back-to-back in silence. Then the next prompt is provided. You may modify this protocol by switching partners between each question.

Blinky Blink: When students get stuck and need a reset, this protocol helps them to consciously shift to see the problem with fresh eyes. They simply blink a set number of times, directing their mental focus away from the scenario. After blinking, they take on the problem or scenario from a new perspective or return their thinking back to the beginning to rethink it. Blinky Blink and the Through Their Eyes protocol work nicely in combination.

Brain Dump: To prepare for conversations, have students activate previous learning with a brain dump. Give students a learning focus then ask them to write everything they can think of that relates to that topic. This brain dump searches for prior knowledge students bring to the lesson and helps refresh their memories by recalling information from a previous lesson.

Carousel: When a lesson calls for students to review multiple pieces of information, bring movement into the lesson by posting segments around the class and creating stations. Small groups move from station to station, gathering information from each source and documenting it on a recording sheet. After they visit a set number of stations, groups analyze the information, create a synthesis, look for patterns, or process it in another way.

Chalk Talk: On a single sheet of large paper, students brainstorm ideas based on a provided prompt or question. After sufficient think time, ask them to communicate and interact with the ideas but only in writing on the chart paper. They must stay silent. Provide each student with a different color marker so you can monitor the interactions between students to be sure everyone is equally represented.

Choral Response: Pose a question to the entire class or group and have them reply in unison. A visual cue is helpful. You can put your hands up to indicate that students should think and wait for a signal. When you drop your hands, students share their thoughts. Use this protocol only when answers are short and have a single correct answer. It works great for vocabulary words or fill-in-the-blank types of questions.

Clock Partners: To save you time in finding partners, set them up in advance. Using a clock face, pair up students with similar skills, interests, or backgrounds for easy differentiation. For example, 6:00 Partners may have similar reading levels. Note: you don't have to have twelve Clock Partner sets. You can use any number of appointment times. Then, when you want to launch a protocol, just say, "Find your 9:00 Partner." (Free downloadable Clock Partner sheet.)

Conga Lines: Students form two lines facing one another. They engage in dialogue with the person in front of them. When time is up, one line moves to the left or right so everyone has a new partner. This can also be done with inner and outer circles (see the Around the Clock protocol).

Done and Run: Gather multiple problems, examples, or excerpts for students to review. Print them on cards or link them to QR codes and number them, then place the cards in a central location in the classroom. Be sure you have more than you need students to complete. Provide students with a recording sheet to keep track of their responses. Launch the task by giving each group a different card. Students work through the problem, analyze an example, or discuss a piece of text and document their responses on the recording sheet. When they're done, the Runner returns the card to the class pile and selects a new card the group hasn't reviewed yet. This process continues so students have multiple opportunities to practice skills or gather pieces of evidence until time is up. The groups move at their own pace, causing some groups to have more responses on their sheets than others. End the task when the slowest group is ready to move on. Bring closure to the activity by asking the students to summarize their learning or apply the practiced skill independently (see Hack 6's Hack in Action for an example).

DRE: Use this process for reflection or peer feedback. D represents a Detail that sticks out to them, R prompts them to share their Response to that detail, and E is the Evaluation of how the response impacts their overall learning.

Fan and Pick: Write questions related to your lesson on index cards. Organize students in groups of four. Student one fans the questions out for student two to choose one. The card selected by student two is read to student three, who responds or solves the problem. Student four responds by paraphrasing student three's response or providing feedback. The roles are rotated, and the process is repeated. An added option is to use questions students wrote on yesterday's exit ticket or during a warm-up. Review the questions and select the most relevant ones for the activity.

Fill Your Head: In this brainstorming and summary structure, students individually craft a response to an open-ended prompt. Then they roam the room sharing their responses and listening to the responses of others without writing them down. When their head is "full" of others' ideas, the students go back to their seats and jot down what they heard. They continue to collect responses from others until time is up. Then, groups of two to four students compare all the information they gathered from others to come up with one synthesized response.

Final Word: Highlight key points in a lesson and allow for multiple perspectives with this protocol. First, students share their quotes without any explanation. The other students discuss the given quote while the first student only listens. Set a timer for their dialogue. When the timer goes off, the first student shares why the quote was chosen and responds to the comments made by the other group members during their discussion. Repeat the process until every student in the group gets a final word.

Finger Votes: Groups use this method to reveal students' preferences and move toward consensus. When learners face choices and the group must make a decision, they can weigh votes with their fingers. They give 0–5 votes based on how strongly each group member feels about a specific option. They cannot give the same number of votes to two different options. Therefore, if a student most prefers options C and D, they must decide which one gets four votes and which one gets five votes. The total number of finger votes for each option provides input from every student and considers how strongly they feel about their recommendations.

Four Corners: Label parts of the room with possible responses to your question, such as A/B/C/D, strongly agree/agree/disagree/ strongly disagree, or always/sometimes/rarely/never. After posing a question, invite students to gather in the part of the room that corresponds with their thinking. There, they can have a standing conversation with others who share similar points of view. In this first conversation, they develop their strong arguments and reasoning before they pair up with someone from another corner to discuss how their thinking differs.

Gallery Walks: Individually or, more often, in small groups, students create a visual to show their learning or explain an idea. Invite students to rotate around the room and visit the different learning exhibits. There are many ways to vary the Gallery Walk. Considerations include allowing students to roam and visit the pieces they choose rather than a systematic rotation. Determine if you want the visuals to stand alone or if one person from the group will stay behind to give a short synopsis and answer questions for the visitors.

Give One–Get One: Ask students to brainstorm ideas individually and document them on a paper grid you provide. Students fill in as many boxes as they can and then approach other classmates to give them an idea and get an idea. The learners continue to give and get ideas until their grids are complete.

Glows and Grows: Prepare students to provide quality feedback to one another by offering a protocol where they can note a combination of strengths and areas for improvement. Glows are shared to communicate shining spots in another student's or another group's work. Grows offer constructive criticism to help everyone move to the next level.

Hand Out Answers: Take the focus off getting to the right answer by removing the mystery. Provide students with correct answers so they can focus on the thinking necessary to reach the final conclusion. This is also an option for students to review their work if you need a few extra minutes for another group to finish.

Huddle Up: This strategy can either be planned or used when needed. When the teacher wants to share information, an announcement, or more resources, one student from each group is chosen to gather with the teacher to receive the message or resource. That student returns to the group to communicate what was shared in the huddle. This prevents unnecessary interruptions of productive group work.

I Have–Who Has? Give each student a word to describe or define and a definition or description of another word. The first person in a group begins by saying "who has" then reading the definition or description provided on their card. The classmate who has the word that matches the definition or description speaks next by saying,

"I have (insert word that was just described or defined). Who has (read their definition or description)?" Change this up by varying the size of the group or the number of cards each student has.

I See–You Draw: Situate students so they face in opposite directions. Give one student an image or random shape and the other student a piece of paper and a pencil. Neither partner can see the other. The student with the picture describes it to their partner, who then attempts to replicate the image using only the verbal descriptions provided. Emphasize the power of questions by not allowing the student who's drawing to ask questions the first time but allowing them to in the second round with a new image.

Icon Story: Group members tell a collective story, one person at a time, using a stack of preprinted random images on cards (such as a train, shoes, flag, and volcano). One person begins the story using an image from the pile as inspiration. As the story progresses, team members must intertwine their images into the group's story. For added fun, allow each group to retell their Icon Story to another group or the whole class.

If-Then-By-So: To emphasize the "why" of an if/then scenario, follow it up with a phrase that describes how students will execute a strategy and what results they anticipate. If (name a problem), then (name a strategy), by (describe how to apply the strategy), so (describe the outcome). For example, "IF we do not agree on an idea, THEN widen perspectives BY asking questions like 'What assumptions are being made?' SO given facts can be separated from inferences."

(3-Step) Jigsaw: Foster interdependence and collaboration with a 3-Step Jigsaw. Segment non-sequential tasks into parts. Step 1: Create expert groups to learn about each individual part and provide them opportunities to thoroughly understand a section. Step 2: Assign one student from each section into new teams. Provide time for students to share their learning, stressing that the objective is for everyone to understand all the parts. Step 3: After each part is shared, return students to their expert groups to process how their part fits into the complete picture.

Join a Team: When a group finishes way before the rest of the class, split up its members and disperse them among the remaining groups. Their function can serve as a facilitator (to lead the group without just handing over the answers), a resource (available to support when the group requests assistance), a communication collector (observe how other groups are implementing communication skills and provide them with feedback) or, if the task is different, simply join the other team as an additional team member.

KWL Chart: Students within groups document what they Know about their learning target, what they Want to know or What questions they have, and what they Learned as a result of working together. This is a proven tool and is a great way for students to track the group's progress. Use the "L" section when you assess students individually to be sure everyone walked away with understanding and clarity.

Make an Analogy: Provide a sentence stem for students to compare your learning concept with something else and to explain why they made the comparison. This not only sparks creativity and gives you insight as to the depth of their understanding, but it can also be fun, sometimes adding humor to the lesson. For example: (Provide the concept) is like _____ because _____.

Examples for different grades:

- Lower Elementary: Reading is like brushing your teeth because you have to do it every day.

- Upper Elementary: Martin Luther King Jr. is like a bumblebee because he pollinates his message from person to person no matter what color they are.

- Middle School: Multiplying two negative numbers is like saying, "I don't have no money" because if you don't have none, you must have some.

- High School: Stalin is like the Tin Man because he was heartless.

Math Work-Share: Math buddies or partners team up to review practice problems. If there is disagreement or if both mathematicians have doubts about the same problem, they talk it through together. When one student explains their strategy, the other listens with the purpose of following the thinking process and identifying any errors. Then they switch roles. Both students engage in error analysis, looking for a silly mistake or a bigger misconception.

Numbered Word Summary: When chunking larger pieces of information or processing complex ideas, task students with summarizing them. Limit the number of words they may use in their summary. Six is a good place to start, but feel free to change up the total number of words, keeping it to a minimum. When identifying a big idea, you can even ask students to limit it to a one-word summary. A supportive modification for students who need it is to allow them to write their complete summary first and then underline the number of words from their summary that are most important.

One-Some-One: The three-step activity begins with single students thinking alone, moves them to connect with a group, then returns them to working alone. First, provide time for students to individually prepare before entering into groups. Second, they gather more information, organize ideas, or collaborate with their team. In the third and final step, they return to work on their own, using the experience in their group to enhance their own thinking.

One Word: Each student thinks of one best word that either describes what they are learning or is an important concept. One by one, group members share their words. After one word is shared by a student, the rest of the group discusses why that word is important to their learning. Once every student shares their word, the group or each individual student creates a summary that includes each of the words shared in their group.

One-Up Prioritizing: To reach agreement, students use this kinesthetic strategy to create a moving graph. First, the group identifies what options they have. Then, each option is listed on an index card and laid out on the table. On their own, students mentally or in writing determine their first, second, and third choices, and so on, until they get to their last choice. The first student moves the cards to reflect their prioritizing. If there are four choices, the first choice moves up four positions from the bottom of the table, leaving room for it to continue moving up to the top of the table; the second choice moves three positions up from the bottom of the table; the third choice moves two positions up from the bottom of the table; and the fourth choice moves only one position. After the first student is done, the four choices look like stair steps, but that will soon change after the other partners apply their prioritizing. The second student uses the same process to continue moving the same cards up the table. They find their first choice, which may be different from the first student's choice, and move it four positions up the table. They move on to their second choice, and so on. After every student completes their round, the choice at the very top of the table is the group's highest priority.

Pair Out: As some groups finish, pair up each group member from one group with a student in another group to create a new partnership outside their original group. Encourage them to compare their groups' responses. Not only does this give each student more exposure to various thinking, but it also separates individual group members from their teammates.

Pair-Square: After students have time to discuss a concept with a partner, combine two partner groups to form a square of four students. The first pair shares their thinking with the second pair, and then as a square, they deliberate the multiple ideas or create a synthesis that represents the thinking of both pairs.

Parking Lot: Acclimate students to not having their questions answered immediately by starting a Parking Lot that holds their questions. It can be a physical poster, part of your board, or a digital location for students to park their questions. Periodically review the questions to see if there are common themes where students are uncertain or if there's anything that requires immediate attention (such as desired tools or confusion about the directions). An added benefit of the Parking Lot is that you now have a record of the types of problems that students aren't solving on their own and are quick to hand over to you.

Pick It–Show It: Groups of students have a single set of hold-up cards (ABCD, Agree/Disagree, or similar). Each time you share a prompt or question, the group must select a single response, and everyone must agree. The first team to respond with the correct answer gets a point. Use this modification to change it up a little: instead of groups sitting near one another, they sit in their normal spots away from their group members. Students have their own sets of hold-up cards. When you present a prompt or question, team members show their personal responses. If their individual responses match their other team members' responses, everyone on the team gets a point, no matter how long it takes them to come to a consensus. (Free downloadable hold-up cards.)

Pinball Talk Moves: Encourage students to demonstrate active listening by prefacing a comment with a paraphrase. Before a student adds, builds, or challenges (see the ABC protocol) a peer's thought, they first share a short summary of how they interpreted their peer's words. Then, they may ABC to extend the conversation topic. When a paraphrase does not adequately or accurately represent the first person's message, the first student has the opportunity to clarify their message to avoid confusion or misunderstanding. (Free downloadable Pinball Talk Moves classroom poster.)

Play the Broken Record: Turn the learning target into a question. When you repeat a guiding question over and over, such as, "What impact do weather and erosion have on the Earth?" it redirects your class to the purpose of the task. Groups can also Play the Broken Record to redirect conversations and productivity back to the learning target. Students might have to return to this protocol multiple times along their learning journey.

Post-It Feedback: Bring in peer assessment of group products by having students visit the other groups and comment on their work. Arm them with two different colors of sticky notes: one color for Glows that represent compliments or strengths of a group's product and another color for Grows that offer suggestions for improvement or questions for the group to consider. Extend the task to give feedback on the feedback to make sure you aren't getting a bunch of "good jobs" that don't really offer any specific help. This process is a natural follow-up to a Gallery Walk.

Rank Responses: Each group member chooses three quotes from the text. Individually, the students reflect on their chosen quotes and prioritize them 1-2-3. The criteria for prioritizing can vary, such as key points, most resonating, and biggest "aha." Next, each group member shares their top pick with the group. Collectively, they determine the best of the best and prepare an explanation for why. Call attention to the criterion they used and ask students to share the responses they considered but didn't ultimately choose. How would the unselected responses from the entire group be ranked for quality? What were they missing or why didn't they make the final cut?

Reciprocal Teaching: This protocol assigns students a specific cognitive task when reading. Predictor, Clarifier, Questioner, and Summarizer are roles students play to either highlight the assigned perspective or facilitate a dialogue related to that point of view. (Free downloadable sample questions and math examples.)

Red, Yellow, Green Light: As they gather information, prompt students or encourage them to prompt themselves to pause and consider how the information meshes with their thinking. This slows them down and directs them to check assumptions for alignment. Red Lights signify information or events that conflict with their thinking, stopping them in their tracks. Yellow Lights indicate something interesting or new that requires them to pause and sparks reflection or connection. Green Lights affirm previous knowledge and suggest the group is ready to move on with its learning.

Rinse and Repeat: This is intended to be short and sweet. Each student on a team takes a turn to quickly share comments about the learning and should be succinct in their thoughts. No cross-talk is allowed. Use this to check for understanding and to summarize learning so far within a lesson or as a lesson closure.

See-Think-Wonder: Students use the process to articulate their thinking and share it with their group. They begin by identifying what they See or notice; oftentimes it's a piece of text, but it also can be a visible observation. Then they narrate what they Think: what connections they make to what they see. Finally, they share what they Wonder or are curious about. The three-part sequence brings metacognitive attention to students' thoughts.

Shared Note-Taking: To process information and aid in comprehension, each learner gathers notes individually before sharing with the group. One at a time, each team member shares their notes. Students can either share verbally while the other group members take notes, or the other group members can see and use the speaker's notes. Once everyone shares, the group generates a summary of everyone's notes.

Silent Choice: When a group must come to an agreement, each member privately writes down their choices and then they simultaneously reveal all their choices. If the group agrees that this strategy will be used to vote, then they choose the option written most often. However, the strategy may also be used to initiate a conversation about why group members prefer A over B, or they can collectively explore the pros and cons of each preference shared within their group.

Spend a Buck: In order to prioritize ideas or concepts, students allocate amounts of money totaling a dollar among choices the group faces. The higher the amount, the more preferred the option. For example, if there are four choices, a student might spend 50 cents for option one, 15 cents for option two, 30 cents for option three, and 5 cents for option four. Consider using this when there are multiple possible answers. (Which response is worth the most cash?) Modify this protocol for younger students by allocating a number of manipulatives like bingo chips instead of money. Another example is using Spend a Buck to help students make choices. (How would you Spend a Buck to present your information: making a video, presenting a skit, or drawing a visual representation?)

Standing Poll: When you ask a question, tell students to stand when they agree with a response. Then they can pair up with others who share their same point of view or compare thinking with someone who stood for a different response.

Stir the Class: Start students in groups of three to five members and assign each student a number. Provide a topic related to the learning for the students to discuss. After students have had sufficient time to discuss the topic, announce a number within their group. The student assigned to that number rotates to a new group and summarizes group one's thinking to group two. This person is now a member of the second group. Pose another discussion item for groups to discuss and repeat the sequence, choosing a different student number to rotate. To keep it random, use a die or a spinner to choose the student number selected to move to a new group.

Through Their Eyes: Expand students' perspectives by challenging them to consider different points of view for a tangible item, problem, or scenario. First, identify what students will analyze, such as a tree. Then list the different perspectives you'd like them to consider and label chairs or provide cards for each. For the tree example, these might include hikers, furniture companies, birds, and air. Students either sit in the chairs or draw cards to choose their perspective. To the group, they then discuss that point of view, such as how hikers, furniture companies, birds, or air view trees. If a group member has something to add, they should sit in that chair or hold that card. The group collectively or individually then combines all the perspectives into one summary. Wrapping up our tree example, they may summarize the various impacts a tree has on the environment. This works with an endless array of topics, such as historical events, social scenarios, characters in a text, and positions on a sports team.

Triad: Assign three partners as A, B, and C. Prepare three open-ended questions that make students reflect or give extended responses. Each question is one round. In the first round, partner A responds to the inquiry, partner B uses the active listening skills of questioning and paraphrasing to keep the conversation going, and partner C observes, listens, and takes notes. After a specified period of time (start with 1 minute and work up/down from there), stop the conversation between partners A and B. Turn the floor to partner C to summarize what they heard. Give partner C half the time that partners A and B had to talk. In round two, share a new question and rotate the roles. The final rotation happens in round three, which provides everyone an opportunity to serve each role.

Turn and Ask: Instead of turning and talking to their partner, students begin their dialogue with a question you provide. When the first partner asks, it guarantees each person has an opportunity to say something, even if it is just posing the question. As your students get more skilled at developing quality questions, invite them to ask their own questions.

Walk and Stop: Challenge listening and thinking skills with this fun activity. Begin with students walking when the leader says "walk" and stopping when the leader says "stop." Then switch the commands. "Walk" means to stop and "stop" means to walk. Make it even more challenging by adding other commands like "hop" and "clap" and then switch those, too.

What's That Noise? To sharpen listening skills, play sounds and have students identify them. Try sounds like water boiling, a specific app alert, someone typing on a keyboard, or jingling keys. An alternate application of this protocol is to play a song and invite students to isolate a specific instrument. It's usually easiest to start with percussion. Play the song for a minute or two and have students see how long they can listen to just the drums without their ears being drawn to other instruments or lyrics.

Word-Phrase-Sentence: This protocol works best with smaller collaborative groups of two to four students. Each student chooses a word, phrase, and sentence that resonates with them related to the learning. Each student shares their word, followed by a group discussion about all the words provided. Next, students share their selected phrase one at a time. Again, follow with a group discussion. Finally, the learners share their sentences with or without cross-talk in between each share.

SNEAK PEEK

THE HACK:

THINK, LEARN, AND COMMUNICATE BY CREATING COMICS

A CCORDING TO YALE researcher Jeffrey Wammes, when we draw, we integrate three distinct types of experiences: semantic (translating words and ideas into visuals), motor (planning hand movements), and visual (watching our drawing appear). The multisensory experience allows us to retrieve more aspects of recording and processing than if we engaged fewer senses like we do when reading or writing.

Wammes's 2016 study demonstrated a phenomenon called "the drawing effect," referring to the significant increase in vocabulary recall when participants drew representative visuals as opposed to only using writing and reading. Recalling one small detail or aspect allows us to reconstruct a full picture. In her influential synthesis of supporting research, biology professor Kim Quillin confirmed that students learn more from combining verbal and visual information than from verbal information alone.

If drawing has such significant learning benefits, we must integrate it into a full academic experience. We can equip students with basic tools to build confidence in drawing. We can give them permission to use various methods to process and express thinking. We can ignite an interest in a topic by appealing to the diverse skills of students who are often disengaged when modes of learning do not vary or leverage intuitive thinking.

With its unique combination of words and pictures, comics serve as a compelling medium for students to think, learn, and communicate.

- Structure exercises that encourage students to explore low-stakes comics creation.

- Ease fears by encouraging them to copy the drawings of others.

- Invite students to respond to reading using the comics form.

- Encourage visual notes during a lesson.

- Represent topics, problem-solving, or task completion with a visual narrative.

Math education expert Nell McAnelly explains that a best practice to develop K–12 students' building blocks for abstract mathematical thinking involves moving students from doing to seeing to abstract application. After learning concrete information, we move to a representational phase where we envision steps and processes. If these two building blocks are skipped, students struggle to reach the abstract phase where understanding is flexible enough to enable proficient problem-solving. When a child illustrates countable physical objects in a drawn model, she clarifies ideas, expands her perspective, and opens a pathway to different approaches.

When I tutored high school students in math, I saw struggles with abstract algebra concepts rooted in foundational gaps—they likely missed a connection when learning an essential concept needed to move from the concrete to the abstract in an earlier grade. How could pictorial representation during initial concept engagement have solidified it so they could apply it in new contexts years later?

To clarify, drawing does not need to be realistic, finely rendered, or beautiful for students to benefit cognitively. Representing an idea, concept, or experience through simple, minimalist drawings still requires translating something we hear or read into another form. In the translation process, we make many choices. We think metaphorically when deciding how to capture a word in a visual and choose color, size, thickness, location, angle, perspective, and juxtaposition.

As Quillin's findings make clear, drawing allows us to visualize the patterns, connections, and relationships among discrete elements of complex systems and structures. More specifically, as Jay Hosler explains, comics are a perfect way to mentally model scientific processes because they force us to:

- Sequence essential steps of a process

- Determine essential events by using different details and information

- See the events happening as we draw them from one panel to the next

Drawing comics to represent what we learn helps us organize complex information using a narrative structure. We can build connection and empathy when creating characters and objects that represent abstract principles and systems. We can revisit the idea or lecture before committing to a visual representation.

- How will I symbolize water vapor here?

- How will I show that pressure is escaping?

- What size should I make this atom to show how small it is compared to the nucleus?

Drawing while we learn captures a concept, image, event, or object, freeing up cognitive space so we can begin to think critically. If I draw the neuron and color in the sodium, I don't have to "hold it in my mind," Hosler explains. I am free to critically consider the system as a whole. If I draw a character from Gabriel Garcia Marquez's *One Hundred Years of Solitude*, along with arrows connecting him to other characters spanning generations, I can think critically about relationships and the influences they have on each other. If I roughly sketch negotiable objects in a math problem, I can creatively think about arrangements and relationships.

WHAT YOU CAN DO TOMORROW

Sometime during adolescence, most people stop drawing, fearful of the idea that they can't draw accurately or as well as talented artists. Instead of fearlessly putting marker to paper like young children, changing our goals and stories to match where pens in our unstable hands might lead us, we resist even trying. We think, "Well, I don't know how to draw that," so we don't. As teachers, our first step is to ease anxiety about drawing.

- Teach them to draw in Brunetti style. In his book *Cartooning*, Ivan Brunetti offers an accessible way to draw people using simple shapes and lines. The head and body are two circular shapes. The limbs are straight and curved lines. Then you add a few details to embellish. (Search YouTube for Brunetti style.) Many teachers use exercises from *Cartooning* as lesson openers to increase students' comfort level with errorproof drawing. Some students create self-portraits in the Brunetti style, later putting that self-character into various situations and contexts.

- This style is spare enough for readers to fill it with life on their own, as opposed to being told who they are seeing as if they were looking at a realistically drawn face and body.

- Suggest stick figures. In *Understanding Comics*, Scott McCloud describes the significance of minimalist iconic images, like a circle with two dots and a curve that represents a human face. The face is abstracted to essential elements so readers can fill it up with their own rich details. Instead of specifics, which lead them to associations and ideas of who they are looking at, a spare version allows us to connect and relate to the character in personally relevant ways. Introduce, model, and practice using stick figures—the most abstract way to draw people. The few details and limited context carry much more significance. McCloud calls this "amplification through simplification." With so few lines and details, anything clearly demarcated carries a purpose.

BUY *HACKING GRAPHIC NOVELS*

AVAILABLE AT:
Amazon.com
10Publications.com
and bookstores near you

ABOUT THE AUTHOR

Connie Hamilton earned her Education Specialist degree in Curriculum and Instructional Leadership from Oakland University and has served in the field of education as a teacher, instructional coach, elementary and secondary principal, and district curriculum director.

Connie is an international speaker and presenter. Her keynotes and workshops are known for striking the perfect balance between grounding strategies in research and making them actionable the next day. Connie is a veteran of the Hack Learning family as the author/coauthor of three Times 10 Publications books:

- *Hacking Group Work: 11 Ways to Build Student Engagement, Accountability, and Cooperation with Collaborative Teams*

- *Hacking Questions: 11 Answers that Create a Culture of Inquiry in Your Classroom*

- *Hacking Homework: 10 Strategies that Inspire Learning Outside the Classroom*

Connie takes a big-picture approach when collaborating with school districts internationally to create systems that connect current and new initiatives. Her mission is to consistently build on the knowledge teachers and leaders already have and help them avoid the pressure of having "one more thing" on their full plates.

Often referred to as the Questioning Guru, Connie Hamilton has the unique ability to blend coaching and consulting to guide administrators and teachers through reflection and professional discovery while offering concrete strategies for an amazing learning and growing experience.

Connect with Connie Hamilton:

website:
www.conniehamilton.org
www.hackinggroupwork.com

Email: email@conniehamilton.org
Twitter: @conniehamilton
LinkedIn: www.linkedin.com/in/connie-hamilton

MORE FROM
TIMES 10 PUBLICATIONS

Browse all titles at 10Publications.com

Hacking School Discipline
9 Ways to Create a Culture of Empathy &
Responsibility Using Restorative Justice
By Nathan Maynard and Brad Weinstein

Reviewers proclaim this *Washington Post* Best-
seller to be "maybe the most important book
a teacher can read, a must for all educators,
fabulous, a game changer!" Teachers and pre-
senters Nathan Maynard and Brad Weinstein
demonstrate how to eliminate punishment
and build a culture of responsible students and
independent learners in a book that will become your new blueprint for school discipline.
Twenty-one straight months at #1 on Amazon, *Hacking School Discipline* is
disrupting education like nothing we've seen in decades—maybe centuries.

Even More Hacking Engagement
New Ways to Make Learning Fun for All
Students
By James Alan Sturtevant

If you and your students aren't approaching
your class each day with excitement for the new
ideas and learning surprises you're about to experience, then it's time to hack your student engagement. This four-decade veteran classroom
teacher knows how to engage learners, and he's
sharing his best ideas with you. Author James
Sturtevant wrote *Hacking Engagement* and
Hacking Engagement Again, and now he's back with 50 new ways to make
the classroom fun for everyone. When you apply Sturtevant's strategies, your
class will become the one they don't want to miss. It's time to engage.

Browse all titles at 10Publications.com

Hacking Questions

11 Answers that Create a Culture of Inquiry in Your Classroom

By Connie Hamilton

Questions are the driving force of learning in classrooms, but teachers have questions about how to engage their students with the art of questioning. *Hacking Questions* digs into framing, delivering, and maximizing questions in the classroom to keep students engaged in learning. Known in education circles as the "Questioning Guru," Connie Hamilton shows teachers of all subjects and grades how to ask the questions that deliver not just answers but reflection, metacognition, and real learning.

Project Based Learning

Real Questions. Real Answers. How to Unpack PBL and Inquiry

By Ross Cooper and Erin Murphy

Educators would love to leverage project based learning to create learner-centered opportunities for their students, but why isn't PBL the norm? Because teachers have questions. *Project Based Learning* is Ross Cooper and Erin Murphy's response to the most common and complex questions educators ask about PBL and inquiry, including: How do I structure a PBL experience? How do I get grades? How do I include direct instruction? What happens when kids don't work well together? Learn how to teach with PBL and inquiry in any subject or grade.

Browse all titles at 10Publications.com

Hacking Assessment 2E
10 Ways to Go Gradeless In a Traditional Grades School
Starr Sackstein

Starr Sackstein is back with an updated road map for educators to hack grading and assessment. Readers will learn about the flaws of traditional assessment systems and how to make immediate changes so students can better advocate for themselves as learners. Begin by addressing your mindset about grading, and learn how to help your community buy into the shift to go gradeless. Bravely change the systems that aren't serving your students.

Hacking Instructional Design
33 Extraordinary Ways to Create a Contemporary Curriculum
By Michael Fisher and Elizabeth Fisher

Whether you want to make subtle changes to your instructional design or turn it on its head—*Hacking Instructional Design* provides a toolbox of options. Discover just-in-time tools to design, upgrade, or adapt your teaching strategies, lesson plans, and unit plans. These strategies offer you the power and permission to be the designer, not the recipient, of a contemporary curriculum. Students and teachers will benefit for years to come when you apply these engaging tools starting tomorrow.

Browse all titles at 10Publications.com

RESOURCES FROM TIMES 10 PUBLICATIONS

10Publications.com

**Nurture your inner educator:
10publications.com/educatortype**

Podcasts:
hacklearningpodcast.com
jamesalansturtevant.com/podcast

On Twitter:
@10Publications
@HackMyLearning
#Times10News
#RealPBL
@LeadForward2
#LeadForward
#HackLearning
#HackingLeadership
#MakeWriting
#HackingQs
#HackingSchoolDiscipline
#LeadWithGrace
#HackingSchoolLibraries

All things Times 10:
10Publications.com

TIMES 10 PUBLICATIONS provides practical solutions that busy educators can read today and use tomorrow. We bring you content from experienced teachers and leaders, and we share it through books, podcasts, webinars, articles, events, and ongoing conversations on social media. Our books and materials help turn practice into action. Stay in touch with us at 10Publications.com and follow our updates on Twitter @10Publications and #Times10News.